Stressed IS JUST Desserts

SPELLED BACKWARDS

A Collection of Great American Desserts

SHERYL MEDDIN *and* BENNETT FRISCH

LONGSTREET PRESS, INC
Atlanta, Georgia

Published by LONGSTREET PRESS, INC.
A subsidiary of Cox Newspapers,
A subsidiary of Cox Enterprises, Inc.
2140 Newmarket Parkway
Suite 122
Marietta, Georgia 30067

Printed in Hong Kong

1st printing 1997

Library of Congress Card Number: 96-79804

ISBN: 1-56352-378-7

Photography by Michael W. Thomas
Book and jacket design by Audrey Graham

We never could have written this cookbook without the invaluable assistance of Stuart Meddin and Michael Burton. Their overactive metabolisms (and sweet tooths) enabled them to sample virtually every recipe we considered, not to mention those requiring testing, retesting and then testing again. Neither ever gained an ounce. Thanks, y'all.

CONTENTS

INTRODUCTION

We opened The Dessert Place in December of 1979. Although variations of the concept have recently become commonplace (witness the profusion of coffee- houses), we were quite an oddity when we began. Back then, the idea of a restaurant/bakery that served only desserts and coffee fascinated people. That reaction always baffled us, because the need for such an establishment just seemed so obvious.

Without being aware of it, the public must have sensed that need. We were fortunate enough to be successful almost from the day we opened our doors. We attribute our success to several factors: (1) our great products, (2) our location in an up-and-coming neighborhood, and (3) our desperation to make the business profitable, thus proving our many naysayers wrong.

Our path was not always an easy one. Without any professional culinary training or restaurant experience, we had a lot of learning to do. Although others considered us "great bakers," making a delicious carrot cake for a friend's birthday is a far cry from producing a 30-plus-item menu on a daily basis. (Not to mention washing the pans, serving the customers, keeping the books, mopping the floors, etc!) At the end of our first day of business — finally closing the store at around midnight — it was frightening to realize that we had to start all over again early the next morning. Somehow, we managed.

That was about 18 years ago. In the meantime, we've had curious customers ask us hundreds of questions. But the four that are most often asked are:

How did you get started in this business?

It was a fluke. Both of us were dissatisfied with our jobs. Both of us wanted our own business. Both of us loved desserts. Then one evening, after a movie, we decided we wanted something sweet. We went to a nearby restaurant, sat down, and ordered dessert. Our waiter looked at us like we were villains, taking up his valuable table and ordering just dessert and coffee. In discussing his indignation, the idea of a dessert restaurant was born.

Where did you get your recipes?

From everyone and everywhere. Just mention dessert and everyone wants to tell you about his/her favorite. The unsolicited recipes ranged from the simple (Rice Krispie squares) to the sublime (Kahlua soufflé with chocolate sauce). We tried them all. (Well, most of them.) Many of them became favorites of ours and appear regularly on The Dessert Place menu. We can't imagine the holiday season without Ellen's Fruitcake Cookies or an Easter without Vivi's Coconut Cake.

How do you stay so skinny?

We don't. We are classic examples of the "yo-yo" syndrome. Whenever our customers stopped asking us this question, we stopped eating.

Why don't you write a cookbook?

Well, we just never had time. However, in June, 1996, we stepped down as owners of The Dessert Place and began to fulfill our final customer request: the compilation of this cookbook. Leaving our business in the capable hands of Meg Moore and Robert Furrey, two of our longtime and dedicated staff members, we then became available to actually commit these recipes to paper, adapting them to portions suitable for home use.

At any rate, in reading this cookbook, you'll notice that these are not complicated recipes. They don't entail elaborate procedures or advanced techniques. Their success relies on the following basic principles:

1. Use only quality ingredients. Your finished product can be only as good as the original components. Don't skimp.

2. Follow the mixing and baking instructions as stated. This will ensure the proper flavors and textures.

3. And understand, with a light heart, that "*stressed* is just *desserts* spelled backwards."

Helpful Hints

EQUIPMENT

- Have your oven calibrated.

- Know your oven. If the heat is distributed unevenly, be sure to move or rotate your pans accordingly to compensate.

- Use heavy-gauge baking sheets and cake pans when possible. Things will bake more evenly.

- In our homes we use a 5-quart Kitchen Aid electric stand mixer. Although you can use a hand mixer, the stand model gives you freedom to do other tasks while the machine does its own thing. We identify which model to use for each recipe. When a recipe specifies an electric mixer, we are referring to the stand model. When a recipe specifies a hand mixer, we are referring to the hand-held electric variety.

- Invest in parchment paper. Some batters stick to the pans more than others. Lining the pans with parchment paper, then greasing and flouring the paper, makes it easier to get the stubborn layers out of the pans intact. Also use parchment paper on baking sheets instead of greasing them. You'll be glad when it's time to clean up.

INGREDIENTS

- We use unbleached, presifted, all-purpose flour; unsalted butter; pure vanilla extract; and large eggs.

- We've had great results using these particular brand names: Land O' Lakes unsalted butter, Crisco vegetable shortening, Ghiradelli cocoa, Lindt white chocolate, Quaker Oats, Nellie & Joe's Key lime juice, Breakstone or Philadelphia cream cheese, Nestle's semi-sweet chocolate and Baker's unsweetened chocolate.

PROCEDURE

- Baking is chemistry. Unlike cooking, the stated proportions in a baking procedure are very important. Too much improvision and the recipe may not work.

- A little organization really helps! Before you begin, read through the entire recipe to familiarize yourself with the process. Then gather and measure out all of the necessary ingredients.

- Start with your ingredients at room temperature. The mixing process will go much more quickly and the result will be a better product.

- You know what they say about rules and exceptions. When making pie crust, you want the butter, shortening, and liquid as cold as possible!

- Separate eggs while they are still cold and then let them come to room temperature. However, for safety's sake, don't leave them out for more than an hour.

- Crack eggs, individually, into a separate bowl before adding them to a batter. This way, you can avoid any "bad eggs" that might be lurking and also ensure that no shells get by you.

- You can melt chocolate in the microwave, but you must do it very carefully. Stir every 15–20 seconds to prevent burning. Do not overcook or the chocolate will become stiff and dark.

- Scrape down the sides and bottom of the mixing bowl using a rubber spatula, several times while making a batter. It helps to thoroughly combine all of the ingredients.

- Once you've added the flour to a recipe, mix as little as possible. You want to make sure that everything is incorporated, but you do not want to jeopardize the texture of the final product.

- "Knock" the cake pans on your counter a few times after you fill them with the batter and before putting them in the oven. This will help eliminate any air bubbles and makes for a more level cake.

- Things will cook faster and more evenly if you bake them on the center rack in the oven.

- After removing baking sheets from the oven, set them on a wire rack to speed up the cooling process.

- When icing cakes, place the first layer down, the second layer up, and, when applicable, the third layer up. This makes the final product more attractive and structurally stable.

- The easiest way to slice cheesecake is to use fishing line. Hold the line taut over the cake. Pull the line down through the cheesecake and then out at the bottom. Rotate the cheesecake and continue until the entire cake is sliced.

- If your cake icing seems too runny to properly coat the layers, put it in the refrigerator for a while to firm it up. If it's gotten too firm, a few seconds in the microwave will fix the problem.

- When storing baked items, put a piece of waxed paper directly on any cut surface to prevent it from drying out.

- Take the time to enjoy the process. And once again, remember, "Stressed is just desserts spelled backwards."

CAKES

THERE ARE OCCASIONS, LIKE BIRTHDAYS, WHEN NOTHING BUT A FRESHLY BAKED, ICED LAYER CAKE WILL DO. SOMEHOW, CANDLES SEEM TO SHINE THEIR BRIGHTEST WHEN BURNING ATOP A HOMEMADE CAKE.

MOST CAKES ARE BETTER THE DAY AFTER THEY ARE ICED. THAT WAY, THE FLAVORS HAVE TIME TO "MARRY." SO, IF AT ALL POSSIBLE, PLAN AHEAD. BUT DON'T LET THIS FACT TAKE THE SPONTANEITY OUT OF YOUR CAKE BAKING. FEW TREATS ARE MORE REWARDING THAN A FRESHLY BAKED CAKE.

ON MANY OF THESE RECIPES, WE HAVE SUGGESTED SIMPLE GARNISHES TO "DRESS THEM UP." ALTHOUGH THE FLAVORS OF THESE CAKES CERTAINLY SPEAK FOR THEMSELVES, WE ARE THOROUGHLY CONVINCED THAT VISUAL PRESENTATION HAS A TREMENDOUS IMPACT ON THE SENSES. JUST THINK OF GARNISHES AS THE PERFECT ACCESSORIES FOR YOUR CAKE. TRY OUR CARROT CAKE ADORNED WITH MARZIPAN CARROTS OR SUGARED PANSIES ATOP OUR BROWNIE CAKE. BUT DON'T STOP AT OUR SUGGESTIONS; THERE ARE HUNDREDS OF OPTIONS. GO AHEAD, ACCESSORIZE!

OUR LAYER CAKES SERVE AT LEAST 12–14 PEOPLE. OTHERS, LIKE THE LEMON POUND CAKE AND THE MYERS'S RUM CAKE, CAN EASILY ACCOMMODATE 15–20. BUT REGARDLESS OF HOW YOU SLICE THEM, WITH THE EXCEPTION OF CHEESECAKES, PLEASE SERVE THEM ALL AT ROOM TEMPERATURE. THEIR FLAVORS ARE MUCH MORE DISCERNIBLE AND THEIR TEXTURES MORE AGREEABLE.

OH, AND DON'T FORGET THE FUN PART — SHARING THE BATTER AND ICING LEFT ON THE BEATERS.

Recipes

RED VELVET CAKE

*T*HIS IS DEFINITELY A "SOUTHERN THING." WE AVOIDED MAKING THIS CAKE FOR YEARS BECAUSE WE WERE "ANTI" FOOD COLORING. FINALLY, AFTER HUNDREDS OF CUSTOMER REQUESTS, WE GAVE IN. LUCKY FOR US, ONE OF OUR KITCHEN MANAGERS HAD THE PERFECT SOLUTION. THANK YOU, JOHN WARNER, FOR SHARING YOUR MOM'S RECIPE WITH US.

LAYERS

1/2 pound (2 sticks) unsalted butter, room temperature
2 cups granulated sugar

3 large eggs, room temperature   *1 teaspoon salt*
1 teaspoon vanilla extract   *4 tablespoons cocoa*
3 cups all-purpose flour   *1 cup milk*
1 tablespoon baking powder   *1/4 cup red food coloring*

Preheat the oven to 350 degrees. Grease and flour three 8-inch cake pans. Set aside.

Using an electric mixer, cream butter on medium speed until light and fluffy. Add sugar and beat well. Add eggs, one at a time, beating well after each addition. Using a rubber spatula, scrape down the sides of the bowl and add vanilla extract. In a small bowl, combine flour, baking powder, salt, and cocoa. Add the flour mixture to the butter mixture alternately with milk, beginning and ending with flour. Add red food coloring and mix well. Scrape down the sides of the bowl again and beat on low speed for 30 seconds.

Pour the batter evenly into the cake pans. Bake on center rack in oven for approximately 30 minutes or until a cake tester comes out clean. Let the layers cool completely on a wire rack before removing them from the pans. Frost the cake with Universal White Frosting.

FROSTING

1 recipe Universal White Frosting (page 19)
Chocolate shavings (for garnish)

Frost the cake. Garnish generously with chocolate shavings.

Store the cake at room temperature.

Serves 10–14

CARROT CAKE

S HERYL THINKS THAT CHARLESTONIANS ARE WEIRD ABOUT SHARING THEIR RECIPES. SHE INSISTS THAT ONE OF HER REASONS FOR OPENING THE DESSERT PLACE WAS TO GET HER HANDS ON BENNETT'S CARROT CAKE RECIPE. IT IS THE BEST!

LAYERS
2 cups all-purpose flour
2 teaspoons baking soda
1 teaspoon salt
2 cups granulated sugar
1 tablespoon plus 2 teaspoons ground cinnamon
4 large eggs, room temperature
1 1/2 cups vegetable oil
1 pound peeled and grated carrots

Preheat the oven to 350 degrees. Grease and flour two 8-inch cake pans. Set aside.

Using an electric mixer, combine all of the dry ingredients. Add eggs, one at a time, and mix well. Scrape down the sides of the bowl with a rubber spatula and add oil. Mix well on medium speed. Add carrots and mix on low speed until ingredients are well blended.

Pour the batter into the cake pans. Bake on center rack in oven for 35-40 minutes or until a cake tester comes out clean. Let the layers cool completely on a wire rack before removing them from the pans. Then frost the cake.

CREAM CHEESE PECAN FROSTING
8 ounces cream cheese, room temperature
1/4 pound (1 stick) unsalted butter, room temperature
4 cups confectioners' sugar
2 teaspoons vanilla extract
1/2 cup pecan pieces

Using an electric mixer on medium speed, combine the cream cheese and butter. Add sugar and vanilla extract and mix until fluffy. Using a rubber spatula, scrape down the sides of the bowl. Stir in pecan pieces. To ensure the proper consistency, refrigerate the frosting for approximately 1 hour before using.

Store cake at room temperature.

Serves 10–14.

CHOCOLATE CHOCOLATE CAKE

*I*N 1978, WHILE WE WERE TESTING RECIPES IN PREPARATION FOR OPENING OUR FIRST STORE, WE KNEW WE NEEDED AN OUTRAGEOUS CHOCOLATE CAKE. WE OBVIOUSLY SUCCEEDED, AS THIS CAKE REPEATEDLY WINS "BEST CAKE" IN ATLANTA IN AREA PUBLICATIONS, YEAR AFTER YEAR.

LAYERS
6 ounces (1 1/2 sticks) unsalted butter, room temperature
2 1/4 cups light brown sugar, packed
3 large eggs, room temperature
3 ounces unsweetened chocolate, melted and cooled
2 teaspoons vanilla extract
2 cups all-purpose flour
2 teaspoons baking soda
3/4 teaspoon salt
1/2 cup buttermilk
1 cup boiling water

Preheat the oven to 350 degrees. Grease and flour two 8-inch cake pans. Set aside.

Using an electric mixer on medium speed, cream butter and add brown sugar. Continue to beat on medium speed, adding eggs one at a time. Beat until the mixture is light and fluffy, about 5 minutes. Add melted, cooled chocolate and vanilla extract. Using a rubber spatula, scrape down the sides of the bowl to make sure the ingredients are well blended. In a small bowl, combine flour, baking soda and salt. Add the dry ingredients to the batter alternately with buttermilk. On low speed, stir in the boiling water. Scrape down the sides of the bowl again and mix well.

Pour the batter evenly into the prepared cake pans. "Knock" the pans on the counter several times to make sure the batter is evenly distributed and air bubbles are eliminated. Bake on center rack in oven for approximately 35–40 minutes or until a cake tester comes out clean. Let the layers cool on a wire rack for about 20 minutes before removing them from the pans. After they have cooled completely, frost the cake with Chocolate Chocolate Frosting.

CHOCOLATE CHOCOLATE FROSTING

1/4 pound (1 stick) unsalted butter, room temperature
1 tablespoon vegetable shortening
2 cups confectioners' sugar
1/4 cup chocolate syrup
1/2 teaspoon salt
3 ounces unsweetened chocolate, melted and cooled
2 teaspoons vanilla extract
1 large egg yolk, room temperature
2 teaspoons hot coffee

Using an electric mixer on medium speed, cream butter and shortening. Add half of the confectioners' sugar and scrape down the sides of the bowl with a rubber spatula. Mix in chocolate syrup. Add remaining sugar, salt, and unsweetened chocolate. Scrape down the sides of the bowl and mix on medium speed for 1 minute. In a small bowl, combine vanilla extract and egg yolk. Pour in hot coffee. Add this vanilla extract/egg mixture to the chocolate mixture. Scrape down the sides of the bowl and mix on high speed for about 2 minutes, or until the frosting is light and fluffy. Refrigerate the icing for about 30 minutes to ensure the proper consistency before frosting the cake.

Store cake at room temperature.

Serves 10–14.

*I*TALIAN CREAM CAKE

*E*XCEPT FOR THE NAME, THERE'S NOTHING ITALIAN ABOUT THIS CAKE. EVEN IF YOU DON'T LIKE COCONUT, GIVE THIS RECIPE A TRY. THE COCONUT IMPARTS MOISTURE, NOT FLAVOR. SEPARATING THE EGGS AND BEATING THE EGG WHITES UNTIL STIFF WILL PREVENT THIS CAKE FROM SINKING SLIGHTLY IN THE CENTER. BUT IF YOU'RE PRESSED FOR TIME OR JUST FEELING LAZY, DON'T BOTHER TO SEPARATE THE EGGS. THE CAKE WILL STILL BE DELICIOUS.

LAYERS
1/4 pound (1 stick) unsalted butter, room temperature
1/2 cup vegetable shortening
2 cups granulated sugar
5 large eggs, separated and room temperature
1 teaspoon vanilla extract
2 cups all-purpose flour
1/2 teaspoon salt
1 teaspoon baking soda
1 cup buttermilk
1 cup sweetened coconut
1 cup pecan pieces

Preheat the oven to 350 degrees. Prepare three 8-inch cake pans by greasing them, lining the bottoms with parchment paper, and greasing the paper. Flour pans and set aside.

Using an electric mixer on medium speed, cream butter and shortening. Add sugar and continue beating until light and fluffy. Add egg yolks, one at a time. Add vanilla extract and mix well. Continue beating until the batter is light and fluffy again. Combine flour, salt, and baking soda and add to the batter, alternately, with buttermilk. Scrape down the sides of the bowl with a rubber spatula and mix on low speed until the batter is smooth. Stir in coconut and pecan pieces. In a medium bowl, using an electric hand-held mixer, beat the egg whites on high speed until stiff and fold them gently into the batter.

Pour the mixture evenly into the cake pans. Bake on center rack in oven for 25–30 minutes or until a cake tester comes out clean. Let the layers cool completely on a wire rack before removing them from the pans and peeling off the parchment paper. Then frost the layers with the Universal White Frosting (page 19).

FROSTING
1 recipe Universal White Frosting (page 19)
1 cup sweetened coconut, toasted (for garnish)

Frost the cake. Garnish generously with the toasted coconut.

Store the cake at room temperature.

Serves 12–16.

Banana Banana Cake

*I*F YOU LIKE BANANAS, YOU'LL LOVE THIS CAKE. WE'VE INCLUDED THE RECIPE FOR BANANA FROSTING, BUT IT IS EQUALLY DELICIOUS ICED WITH EITHER OUR CHOCOLATE CHOCOLATE FROSTING (PAGE 7) OR SWEETENED WHIPPED CREAM FROSTING (PAGE 16).

LAYERS
3 ripe medium bananas, puréed
1/2 cup buttermilk
1 teaspoon vanilla extract
6 ounces (1 1/2 sticks) unsalted butter, room temperature
1 1/2 cups granulated sugar
2 large eggs, room temperature
2 cups all-purpose flour
1 teaspoon baking soda
1 teaspoon baking powder
1/2 teaspoon salt

Preheat the oven to 350 degrees. Prepare two 8-inch cake pans by greasing the pans, lining the bottoms with parchment paper, and greasing the paper. Flour pans and set aside.

Using a food processor fitted with a metal blade, purée the bananas. In a small bowl, combine puréed bananas, buttermilk, and vanilla extract. Using an electric mixer on medium speed, cream butter. Add sugar and beat until light and fluffy, approximately 5 minutes. Beat in eggs, one at a time. Using a rubber spatula, scrape down the sides of the bowl. In another small bowl, combine the dry ingredients and add alternately with the banana mixture to the batter. Mix on low speed, being careful not to overbeat.

Pour the mixture evenly into the cake pans. Knock the pans on the counter to level out the batter and to eliminate any air bubbles. Bake on center rack in oven for 35–40 minutes or until a cake tester comes out clean. Do not test these layers too early, as it will cause them to sink in the middle. Let the layers cool completely on a wire rack before removing them from the pans. Peel off the parchment paper. Then frost the cake.

BANANA FROSTING
1 ripe small banana, puréed
1/8 pound (1/2 stick) unsalted butter, room temperature
3 cups confectioners' sugar
1 teaspoon vanilla extract
1/2 cup pecan pieces

Using a food processor fitted with a metal blade, purée the banana. Using an electric mixer on medium speed, cream butter well. Alternately, add confectioners' sugar and puréed banana to the butter. Add vanilla extract and beat well. Scrape down the sides of the bowl with a rubber spatula and stir in pecan pieces. Refrigerate the icing for about 1 hour to ensure the proper consistency before frosting the cake.

Store the cake at room temperature.

Serves 10–14.

Note: For a little added zip, you might want to spread a thin layer of raspberry preserves on the bottom cake layer before icing the cake.

GERMAN CHOCOLATE CAKE

Sheryl's college roommate (from many, many years ago) returned from Christmas vacation with a care package that included a German chocolate cake. It disappeared in no time. Sheryl begged for the recipe and here it is.

LAYERS

4 ounces German sweet chocolate
1/2 cup boiling water
1/2 pound (2 sticks) unsalted butter, room temperature
2 cups granulated sugar
4 large eggs, separated and room temperature
1 teaspoon vanilla extract
2 cups plus 3 tablespoons all-purpose flour
1/2 teaspoon salt
1 teaspoon baking soda
1 cup buttermilk

Preheat the oven to 350 degrees. Prepare three 8-inch cake pans by greasing them, lining the bottoms with parchment paper, and greasing the paper. Flour pans and set aside.

In a small saucepan over low heat, melt chocolate in boiling water and set aside. Using an electric mixer on medium speed, cream butter. Add sugar and continue beating until light and fluffy, approximately 5 minutes. Add egg yolks, one at a time, beating after each addition. Add vanilla extract to the chocolate mixture. Add the chocolate mixture to the batter. In a small bowl, combine flour, salt, and baking soda and add alternately with buttermilk to the chocolate batter. Beat well after each addition. Scrape down the sides of the bowl with a rubber spatula and mix on low speed until the batter is smooth. In a medium bowl, using an electric hand-held mixer, beat the egg whites until stiff peaks form. Carefully fold the egg whites into the batter.

Pour the batter evenly into the pans. Bake on center rack in oven for 35–40 minutes or until a cake tester comes out clean. Cool completely on a wire rack before removing the layers from the pans. Peel off the parchment paper. Then frost the cake.

GERMAN CHOCOLATE FROSTING

1 cup evaporated milk
1 cup granulated sugar
3 large egg yolks, room temperature
1/4 pound (1 stick) unsalted butter, room temperature
1 teaspoon vanilla extract
1/4 teaspoon salt
1 1/2 cups sweetened coconut
1 cup pecan pieces

Combine evaporated milk, sugar, egg yolks, butter, vanilla extract, and salt in a medium saucepan. Cook over medium heat, stirring constantly until the mixture thickens, approximately 12–15 minutes. Remove the pan from the heat and stir in coconut and pecan pieces. Continue stirring until the frosting is cool and thick enough to spread on the cake.

Store the cake in the refrigerator but bring it to room temperature before serving.

Serves 10–14.

Brownie Cake

Some people tend to be possessive about their recipes. We imagine that Elza Alterman of Charleston, South Carolina, just got tired of making this for everyone and decided to share her secret. This is essentially a two-layer chocolate nut brownie with frosting. It is decadence personified!

Layers
1/2 pound (2 sticks) unsalted butter
4 ounces unsweetened chocolate
2 cups granulated sugar
1 teaspoon vanilla extract
4 large eggs, room temperature
1 cup all-purpose flour
1 teaspoon salt
2 cups pecan pieces

Preheat the oven to 350 degrees. Prepare two 8-inch cake pans by greasing them, lining the bottoms with parchment paper, and greasing the paper. Flour the pans. Set aside.

In a small saucepan over low heat, combine and melt butter and chocolate. Using an electric mixer on low speed, combine the butter and chocolate mixture with sugar and mix well. Add vanilla extract and eggs, one at a time, beating well between additions and, using a rubber spatula, scrape down the sides of the bowl as necessary. Stir in flour, salt, and pecan pieces. Mix on low speed until combined.

Pour the batter evenly into the pans, knock the pans on the counter to level the batter and eliminate any air bubbles, and bake on center rack in oven for 30 minutes or until a cake tester comes out clean. Let the layers cool in the pans on a wire rack for 15 minutes and then remove from pans. Carefully peel the paper off the layers. Let the layers cool completely on a wire rack before frosting the cake.

CHOCOLATE SILK FROSTING

1/4 pound (1 stick) unsalted butter, room temperature
1/2 cup cocoa
6 cups confectioners' sugar
2 teaspoons vanilla extract
1/4 cup half and half

Using an electric mixer on medium speed, cream butter well. Add cocoa and confectioners' sugar. Scrape down the sides of the bowl with a rubber spatula and continue beating until well combined. Add vanilla extract. Slowly add half and half, using just enough to achieve a creamy, spreadable consistency. Frost the cake.

Store the cake at room temperature.

Serves 12–16.

STRAWBERRIES AND CREAM CAKE

*A*T THE HEIGHT OF STRAWBERRY SEASON, NOTHING SHOWS THEM OFF AS WELL AS THIS CAKE. GARNISHING THE PLATTER WITH CHOCOLATE-DIPPED STRAWBERRIES MAKES IT A BEAUTIFUL PRESENTATION.

LAYERS
1 Universal White Cake (page 18)

Prepare layers of Universal White Cake.

SWEETENED WHIPPED CREAM FROSTING
1 1/2 pints (3 cups) whipping cream, chilled
2 tablespoons plus 2 teaspoons confectioners' sugar
3/4 teaspoon vanilla extract
1 1/2 pints fresh strawberries, thinly sliced
1/2 pint fresh strawberries, whole (for garnish)

Using an electric mixer on high speed, beat the whipping cream, confectioners' sugar, and vanilla extract until stiff.

To assemble the cake, cover the bottom cake layer with 1 cup of the Sweetened Whipped Cream Frosting. Arrange the thinly sliced strawberries over the first layer, pressing them into the whipped cream. Top with the second cake layer and repeat the process. Top with the third cake layer. Frost the sides and top of the cake with the remaining frosting.

Slice the remaining strawberries in half and decorate the top and/or sides of the cake.

Store the cake in the refrigerator but bring it to room temperature before serving.

Serves 12–16.

Note: For a little extra zing, you might want to brush the cake layers with Grand Marnier. It's certainly not necessary, but it sure is good.

Coconut Cake

*T*HIS RECIPE CAME FROM VIVI JOHNSON (BENNETT'S EX-MOTHER-IN-LAW) AND QUICKLY BECAME THE FAVORITE OF OUR DEAR FRIEND GEDDINGS ARTHUR (YES — FIRST NAME GEDDINGS, LAST NAME ARTHUR). HE ORDERS THIS CAKE FOR EVERY SPECIAL OCCASION. NOW THAT WE'VE PUBLISHED THE RECIPE, HE CAN HAVE IT ANY TIME HE WANTS IT.

LAYERS
1 Universal White Cake (page 18)

Prepare layers of Universal White Cake.

LEMON FILLING

1 cup granulated sugar	*4 egg yolks, room temperature and lightly beaten*
1/4 cup cornstarch	*1/3 cup freshly squeezed lemon juice*
1 cup boiling water	*2 tablespoons unsalted butter, room temperature*

Combine sugar and cornstarch in a medium saucepan. Stir in water. Cook over medium heat, stirring constantly, until sugar and cornstarch dissolve. Gradually stir about 1/4 of the hot mixture into egg yolks. Then add yolks to remaining hot mixture, stirring constantly with a whisk. Add lemon juice. Continue whisking until the mixture thickens, about 5 minutes. Remove from heat and add butter. Continue to stir the mixture as it cools.

COCONUT FROSTING

2 cups granulated sugar	*2 cups sweetened coconut*
2 cups sour cream	*Additional coconut (for garnish)*

In a large bowl, using a wooden spoon, combine all ingredients.

To assemble the cake, spread a thin layer of the Coconut Frosting on the first layer and then spread half of the lemon filling over it. Top with the second layer and repeat the process. Top with the third cake layer and frost the top and sides of the cake with the Coconut Frosting.

Garnish the cake with the additional coconut to achieve a more finished look.

Store the cake in the refrigerator but bring it to room temperature before serving.

Serves 12–16.

UNIVERSAL WHITE CAKE

*T*O SOME PEOPLE, THE "ONLY" BIRTHDAY CAKE IS THIS WHITE LAYER CAKE, ICED WITH EITHER OUR UNIVERSAL WHITE FROSTING OR OUR CHOCOLATE CHOCOLATE FROSTING. BUT TO US, THIS CAKE HAS BECOME THE BASIS FOR TWO OF OUR FAVORITES: STRAWBERRIES AND CREAM CAKE AND COCONUT CAKE.

LAYERS
1/2 pound (2 sticks) unsalted butter, room temperature
2 cups granulated sugar
4 large eggs, separated and room temperature
1 teaspoon vanilla extract
3 cups all-purpose flour
1 tablespoon baking powder
1 cup milk
1/4 teaspoon salt

Preheat the oven to 350 degrees. Grease and flour three 8-inch cake pans. Set aside.

Using an electric mixer on medium speed, cream the butter well. Gradually add sugar and beat well. Add egg yolks, one at a time, scraping down the sides of the bowl with a rubber spatula. Beat until light and fluffy, about 5 minutes. Add the vanilla extract. In a small bowl, combine flour and baking powder and add to the batter alternately with the milk. Scrape down the sides of the bowl and beat on low speed until just blended. In a medium bowl, using an electric hand-held mixer on high speed, beat egg whites with salt until stiff peaks form. Stir about one-half of the egg whites into the batter. Gently fold in the remainder of the egg whites.

Pour the batter into the cake pans. Bake on center rack in oven for 18–22 minutes or until a cake tester comes out clean. Cool completely on a wire rack before removing the layers from the pans.

Frost the cake with Universal White Frosting (facing page). Store at room temperature.

Serves 10–14.

UNIVERSAL WHITE FROSTING

*T*HIS BASIC WHITE FROSTING HAS PROVEN TO BE VERY VERSATILE OVER THE YEARS! AS TASTY AS A BUTTER CREAM, AS STURDY AS A "ROYAL" ICING, IT HOLDS UP TO ALMOST ANY FLAVOR CAKE WITHOUT OVERPOWERING IT.

8 ounces cream cheese, room temperature
1/4 pound (1 stick) unsalted butter, room temperature
4 cups confectioners' sugar
2 teaspoons vanilla extract

Using an electric mixer on medium speed, beat cream cheese and butter. Add the confectioners' sugar one cup at a time, scraping down the sides of the bowl with a rubber spatula and beating until smooth. Add vanilla extract. Beat the frosting until light and fluffy.

Refrigerate frosting for approximately 1 hour before using to ensure proper spreading consistency.

KEY LIME CHEESECAKE

*T*HE TEXTURE OF CHEESECAKE AND THE PUCKER OF KEY LIMES! STUART MEDDIN (SHERYL'S HUSBAND) PROCLAIMS THIS HIS FAVORITE OF FAVORITES.

CRUST
1 1/4 cups graham cracker crumbs
2 tablespoons granulated sugar
1/8 pound (1/2 stick) unsalted butter, melted

Preheat the oven to 325 degrees. Combine graham cracker crumbs and sugar in a small bowl. Add the melted butter and mix well. Using your fingertips, press the crumb mixture into the bottom of a 9-inch springform pan. Bake crust on center rack in oven for 7–10 minutes and set aside.

Reduce the oven temperature to 300 degrees.

FILLING
2 pounds (4 8-ounce packages) cream cheese, room temperature
1 1/3 cups granulated sugar
2 tablespoons all-purpose flour
1 teaspoon vanilla extract
5 large eggs, room temperature
2 large egg yolks, room temperature
1/2 cup Key lime juice
2 tablespoons heavy cream

Using an electric mixer on medium speed, cream the cream cheese. Add sugar, flour, and vanilla extract. Beat well, on low speed, scraping down the sides of the bowl with a rubber spatula. DO NOT WHIP. Add eggs and egg yolks, one at a time, beating well after each addition. Add Key lime juice. Scrape down the sides of the bowl and add the heavy cream. Blend thoroughly on low speed.

Pour the batter into the prepared crust and bake on center rack in oven for 1 1/4–1 3/4 hours, or until the center of the cake is set.

Let the cake cool on a wire rack at least 2 hours at room temperature. Refrigerate overnight before removing from the springform pan.

Garnish with thin slices of Key limes or grated lime rind.

Store the cheesecake in the refrigerator until ready to serve.

Serves 10–12.

CHOCOLATE WHITE CHOCOLATE CHEESECAKE

T SEEMS WE HAVE MADE EVERY CHEESECAKE FLAVOR IMAGINABLE. BY VARYING THE CRUST, FILLING, AND TOPPING, THE POSSIBILITIES BECOME ENDLESS. THIS PARTICULAR COMBINATION COMMANDS ATTENTION. DELICIOUS AND BEAUTIFUL.

CRUST
9-ounce package chocolate wafer cookies
1/8 pound (1/2 stick) unsalted butter, melted

Preheat oven to 325 degrees.

In a food processor fitted with a metal blade, process the chocolate wafers. Add melted butter and mix well. Using your fingertips, press the crumbs into the bottom of a 9-inch springform pan. Bake crust on the center rack in oven for 7–8 minutes. Set aside.

Reduce oven temperature to 300 degrees.

FILLING
2 pounds (4 8-ounce packages) cream cheese, room temperature
1 1/3 cups granulated sugar
2 tablespoons all-purpose flour
1 teaspoon vanilla extract
5 large eggs, room temperature
2 large egg yolks, room temperature
6 ounces white chocolate, chopped into small pieces
2 tablespoons heavy cream

Using an electric mixer on medium speed, cream the cream cheese. Add sugar, flour, and vanilla extract. Beat well on low speed, scraping the sides of the bowl with a rubber spatula. DO NOT WHIP. Add eggs and yolks, one at a time, beating well after each addition. Add the white chocolate pieces and blend. Stir in the heavy cream.

Pour the batter into the prepared crust and bake for 1 1/4–1 3/4 hours or until the center of the cake is set.

Let the cheesecake cool on a wire rack at least 2 hours at room temperature. Refrigerate overnight before removing from the springform pan. After removing the cheesecake from the pan, top with the chocolate glaze.

CHOCOLATE GLAZE
1 cup semi-sweet chocolate chips, melted
3 tablespoons sour cream
White chocolate shavings (for garnish)

In a small saucepan over very low heat, melt chocolate chips. Blend sour cream into the melted chocolate. Mix until chocolate has a dark, shiny appearance. Spread the glaze over the top of the cheesecake and garnish generously with white chocolate shavings.

Store the cheesecake in the refrigerator until ready to serve.

Serves 10–12.

CHOCOLATE ROULADE

"Beautiful," a.k.a. Renee Frisch (Bennett's mom), makes this dessert whenever she is asked to contribute to a meal. We never really know whether it is because everyone loves it or because it is the only thing she can bake. Regardless, this roulade is a delicious, "Beautiful" dessert.

CAKE
8 *large eggs, separated and room temperature*
1/2 *cup granulated sugar*
1/2 *cup cocoa*
1 *teaspoon vanilla extract*
1/4 *teaspoon salt*

Preheat the oven to 350 degrees.

Prepare a 15 x 10 x 1-inch jellyroll pan by greasing it, lining it with parchment paper, and greasing the paper. Then dust the paper lightly with cocoa. Set aside.

Using an electric mixer on medium speed, beat egg yolks well. Gradually add sugar and beat until the mixture is a light lemon color, approximately 5 minutes. Slowly add cocoa and vanilla extract. Using a rubber spatula, scrape down the sides of the bowl, mix well, and set the batter aside. In a large bowl, using an electric hand-held mixer on high speed, beat egg whites until foamy. Add salt and continue beating until stiff peaks form. Carefully fold egg whites into the cocoa mixture.

Pour the batter into the prepared pan. Lightly tap the pan on the counter to distribute the batter evenly and eliminate any air bubbles. Bake on center rack in oven for 15–20 minutes or until a cake tester comes out clean. Let the cake cool on a wire rack for 10 minutes.

Dust a clean, large kitchen cloth with 3–4 tablespoons of cocoa. Turn the cake out onto the towel. Peel off the parchment paper. Beginning with short end, roll the cake layer, along with the towel, in a jellyroll style. Let the cake cool completely rolled up in this fashion before filling the roulade, approximately 30 minutes.

After the cake has cooled, unroll the layer. At this point, you've got options galore:

1. Top the layer with Sweetened Whipped Cream Frosting (page 16).
2. Brush the layer with the liqueur of your choice, and top with Sweetened Whipped Cream Frosting (page 16).
3. Top the layer with Chocolate Chocolate Frosting (page 7).
4. Try any combination of the above.
5. Try any combination that strikes your fancy.

Roll the cake back up (without the cloth), ending with the seam side down. If desired, frost the finished roulade with Sweetened Whipped Cream Frosting.

Refrigerate the roulade until ready to use. If you opt not to frost the finished roulade, dust it lightly with powdered sugar before serving. After slicing, consider the addition of your favorite hot fudge sauce!

Serves approximately 10.

Note: This flourless dessert is the perfect ending to a Passover dinner!

PUMPKIN ROULADE

*I*F YOU ARE LOOKING FOR SOMETHING DIFFERENT FOR YOUR THANKSGIVING DESSERT, GIVE THIS A TRY. IT OFFERS THE TRADITION OF PUMPKIN IN A NON-TRADITIONAL FORMAT.

CAKE

4 large eggs, room temperature
1 cup granulated sugar
2/3 cup pumpkin (yes, canned is OK!)
1 1/2 teaspoons lemon juice
3/4 cup all-purpose flour
1 teaspoon baking powder
1/2 teaspoon salt
2 teaspoons ground cinnamon
1 teaspoon ground nutmeg
1 teaspoon ground ginger
4 tablespoons confectioners' sugar, for dusting

Preheat the oven to 375 degrees. Grease and flour a 15 x 10 x 1-inch jellyroll pan. Set aside.

Using an electric mixer on high speed, beat eggs on high speed until foamy. Gradually add sugar, beating until frothy. On medium speed, blend in pumpkin and lemon juice. In a small bowl, combine flour, baking powder, salt, cinnamon, nutmeg, and ginger. Add dry ingredients to the pumpkin mixture, scraping down the sides of the bowl with a rubber spatula, and beat until combined.

Pour the batter into the jellyroll pan. Tap the pan on the counter top to ensure the batter is evenly distributed and that any air bubbles are eliminated. Bake on center rack in oven for 15–20 minutes, or until a cake tester comes out clean. Let the cake cool on a wire rack for 10 minutes.

Dust a clean, large kitchen towel with 3–4 tablespoons of confectioners' sugar. Turn the cake out onto the towel. Beginning with short end, roll up the cake, along with the towel, in a jellyroll style. Let the cake cool completely rolled up in this fashion before filling the roulade, approximately 30 minutes.

LEMON WALNUT FILLING

1/8 pound (1/2 stick) unsalted butter, room temperature
8 ounces cream cheese, room temperature
1 3/4 cups confectioners' sugar
2 teaspoons freshly squeezed lemon juice
Grated rind of 1 large lemon
1 cup chopped walnuts

Using an electric mixer on high speed, cream butter, cream cheese, and sugar until light and fluffy, scraping down the sides of the bowl with a rubber spatula. Add lemon juice and rind. Scrape down the bowl and beat well again. Stir in walnuts.

When the cake is cool, gently unroll it and spread the filling evenly over the entire cake. Roll the cake up (without the towel), ending with the seam side down.

Refrigerate the roulade until ready to use. Before serving, dust the roll with powdered sugar.

Serves 10–12.

QUAKER OATMEAL CAKE

JEROME WILLIAMS (OUR VERY FIRST EMPLOYEE) GAVE US THIS RECIPE SHORTLY AFTER WE OPENED THE DESSERT PLACE. ONE OF HIS CHILDHOOD FAVORITES, THIS SPICY OATMEAL-BASED CAKE IS BAKED TWO TIMES, THE FIRST TIME FOR THE CAKE AND THE SECOND TIME FOR THE TOPPING!

CAKE

1 cup Quaker quick oats
1 1/4 cups boiling water
1/2 cup vegetable shortening
1 cup light brown sugar, packed
1 cup granulated sugar
2 large eggs, room temperature
1 teaspoon vanilla extract
1 1/4 cups all-purpose flour
1 teaspoon baking soda
1/2 teaspoon salt
1/2 teaspoon ground cinnamon
1/2 teaspoon ground nutmeg

Preheat the oven to 350 degrees. Grease and flour a 9-inch springform pan. Set aside.

In a small bowl, combine the oats with the boiling water. Let the mixture stand 10 minutes. Using an electric mixer on medium speed, cream the shortening. Add both sugars and mix well. Add eggs, one at a time, and vanilla extract. Continue beating until light and fluffy. Add the oatmeal mixture and combine well, scraping down the sides of the bowl with a rubber spatula. In a small bowl, combine the dry ingredients and stir them into the mixture.

Pour the batter into the springform pan. Bake on center rack in oven for 40–45 minutes until almost done. Cake will still be gooey in center when tested. Remove cake from the oven and spread the topping over the hot cake.

TOPPING

1/4 pound (1 stick) unsalted butter, melted and cooled
1 cup light brown sugar, packed
1 cup sweetened coconut
1 cup pecan pieces
1/2 teaspoon salt
2 large egg yolks, room temperature
2—4 teaspoons milk

Using an electric mixer on low speed, combine brown sugar with coconut, pecans, and salt. On medium speed add egg yolks and beat well. Add melted and cooled butter and mix until well combined. If needed, add a small amount of milk to make the topping a more spreadable consistency.

Spread the topping over the cake and bake on center rack in oven for an additional 18—22 minutes or until golden brown. Let the cake cool completely on a wire rack before removing it from the pan.

Store the cake at room temperature.

Serves 10—12.

POPPY SEED LOAF

*N*OT ONLY IS THIS A GREAT LOAF CAKE, IT MAKES OUTRAGEOUS FRENCH TOAST!

1/2 cup poppy seeds
3/4 cup milk
6 ounces (1 1/2 sticks) unsalted butter, room temperature
1 1/4 cups granulated sugar
3 large eggs, room temperature
1 1/4 teaspoons vanilla extract
2 cups all-purpose flour
2 teaspoons baking powder
1/2 teaspoon salt
Confectioners' sugar for garnish

In a small bowl, combine the poppy seeds with the milk. Let the mixture stand at room temperature for 1 hour.

Preheat oven to 350 degrees. Grease and flour an 8 1/2 x 4 1/2 x 2 1/2-inch loaf pan. Set aside.

Using an electric mixer on medium speed, cream butter. Add sugar and continue to beat until light and fluffy. Using a rubber spatula, scrape down the sides of the bowl and add eggs, one at a time, and vanilla extract. In a small bowl, combine dry ingredients and, on low speed, add alternately to the batter with the milk/poppy seed mixture.

Pour the batter into the pan and knock the pan on the counter to eliminate any air bubbles. Bake on center rack in oven for 35–40 minutes, or until the center springs back when lightly pressed with your fingertip. Do not test this cake too early, as it will sink in the middle. Cool the cake completely on a wire rack before turning it out of the pan.

Sprinkle with confectioners' sugar, if desired.

Store the loaf at room temperature.

Serves 8–10.

"Knock" the cake pans on your counter a few times after you fill them with the batter and before putting them in the oven. This will help eliminate any air bubbles and makes for a more level cake.

GINGERBREAD CAKE

W HEN THE AROMA OF THIS CAKE FILLS YOUR KITCHEN, YOU'LL KNOW THE HOLIDAY SEASON IS APPROACHING. BECAUSE THIS CAKE SEEMS TO GET BETTER BY THE DAY, IT MAKES A GREAT GIFT. IT'S ALSO THE PERFECT TREAT TO HAVE ON HAND FOR UNEXPECTED GUESTS.

LAYER
1 large egg, room temperature
1/2 cup granulated sugar
1/4 pound (1 stick) unsalted butter, melted and cooled
2 1/2 cups all-purpose flour
1 1/2 teaspoons baking soda
1 1/4 teaspoons ground cinnamon
1 1/4 teaspoons ground ginger
1/2 teaspoon salt
1/2 cup dark molasses
1/2 cup honey
1 cup hot water

Preheat the oven to 350 degrees. Grease and flour one 8-inch cake pan. (This is a thin batter and will stick to the pan if it is not greased well.)

Using an electric mixer on medium speed, beat egg and then add sugar, mixing well. On low speed, slowly add melted and cooled butter. In a small bowl, combine flour, baking soda, cinnamon, ginger, and salt. In another small bowl, combine molasses, honey, and hot water. Alternately, add dry and liquid ingredients to the egg/butter mixture. Scrape down the sides of the bowl with a rubber spatula and mix well.

Pour the batter into the cake pan and bake on center rack in oven for 50 minutes, or until a cake tester comes out clean. Let the cake cool completely on a wire rack before removing it from the pan.

You have an option here: to frost or not to frost. If you decide not to frost, this cake is delicious simply heated and sprinkled with confectioners' sugar for a "finished" look. Whipped cream is a good addition. If you opt for a frosted cake, try this:

LEMON FROSTING

4 ounces cream cheese, room temperature
1/8 pound (1/2 stick) unsalted butter, room temperature
2 cups confectioners' sugar
2–4 tablespoons grated lemon rind

Using an electric mixer on medium speed, combine cream cheese and butter. Beat until fluffy. Add sugar and continue to mix until fluffy again. Stir in lemon rind.

Frost the top and/or sides of the cake.

Store the cake at room temperature.

Serves 6–8.

LEMON POUND CAKE

THIS RECIPE COMES COURTESY OF EVE BERLINSKY (SHERYL'S SISTER-IN-LAW). SINCE THE DAY WE PUT IT ON THE MENU AT THE DESSERT PLACE, IT HAS BEEN ONE OF THE BEST SELLERS. TRY IT WITH ICE CREAM, FRUIT PURÉE AND WHIPPED CREAM, OR LAYERED IN A TRIFLE. BECAUSE THIS CAKE IS STURDY AND KEEPS SO WELL, IT'S A GREAT ITEM FOR MAILING.

CAKE
3/4 pound (3 sticks) unsalted butter, room temperature
8 ounces cream cheese, room temperature
1 tablespoon vegetable shortening
3 cups granulated sugar
1 1/2 tablespoons vanilla extract
2 tablespoons lemon juice
Rind of 1 large lemon, grated
6 large eggs, room temperature
3 cups all-purpose flour
1/2 teaspoon salt

Preheat the oven to 350 degrees. Grease and flour a 10-inch tube pan. Set aside.

Using an electric mixer on medium speed, cream butter until very soft. Add cream cheese and shortening and mix on medium speed until light and fluffy, about 5 minutes. Add sugar, vanilla extract, lemon juice, and rind. Beat well. Using a rubber spatula, scrape down the sides of the bowl. Add eggs, one at a time, and beat until light and fluffy again. Add flour and salt, scrape down the sides of the bowl, and mix until flour is thoroughly incorporated.

Pour the batter into the tube pan and bake on center rack in oven for approximately 1 1/4 hours or until a cake tester comes out clean. Cool the cake completely on a wire rack before removing it from the pan. Frost the top of the cake with the Lemon Glaze.

LEMON GLAZE
1 cup confectioners' sugar
1/4 teaspoon vanilla extract
2—4 tablespoons milk

In a small bowl, mix confectioners' sugar and vanilla extract. Add enough milk to make the glaze thin enough to pour, but not too runny!

Pour the glaze over the top of the cake, letting it drip down the sides.

Store the cake at room temperature.

Serves 16—20.

Note: If you are wrapping the cake for mailing, let the glaze set overnight to harden.

Myers's Rum Cake

≈

YOU KNOW THAT RUM CAKE RECIPE YOU ALWAYS SEE THAT CALLS FOR A WHITE CAKE MIX? WE LOVED THAT CONCEPT, BUT COULDN'T BRING OURSELVES TO USE THE MIX. SO, WE CAME UP WITH A "FROM SCRATCH" VERSION OF THIS YUMMY DESSERT!

CAKE
1/2 cup pecan pieces, toasted
1/2 cup almonds, toasted and chopped
1/2 pound (2 sticks) unsalted butter, room temperature
2 cups granulated sugar
4 large eggs, room temperature
3 1/2 cups all-purpose flour
1 tablespoon baking powder
1/2 teaspoon salt
3/4 cup milk
1/2 cup Myers's dark rum

Preheat the oven to 325 degrees. Grease and flour a 10-inch Bundt pan. Set aside.

Sprinkle the nuts evenly over the bottom of the pan. Using an electric mixer on medium speed, cream butter well and add sugar. Add eggs, one at a time, and continue beating until light and fluffy, about 5 minutes. In a small bowl, combine the flour, baking powder and salt and add to the batter alternately with milk. Scrape down the sides of the bowl with a rubber spatula and mix until flour is blended. Do not whip. Slowly stir in rum.

Pour the batter into the Bundt pan and bake on center rack in oven for 1 1/4 hours or until the cake tester comes out clean. Glaze the cake.

Rum Glaze
1 cup light brown sugar, packed
1 cup granulated sugar
2 tablespoons unsalted butter
1/2 cup water
1/2 teaspoon salt
1/2 cup Myers's rum

Combine all of the ingredients, except rum, in a saucepan. Bring the mixture to a boil over medium heat and boil for 4 minutes. Remove from heat and slowly stir in rum.

Pour three-quarters of the glaze over the hot cake while the cake is still in the pan. Let the cake cool completely on a wire rack and then turn it out of the pan. Pour the remainder of the glaze over the top of the cake.

Store the cake at room temperature.

Serves 12—16.

Ann's Pull-Apart Cake
a.k.a. Monkey Bread

*T*HE SECRET TO THIS RECIPE, GIVEN TO US BY ANN HELLMAN (SHERYL'S SISTER-IN-LAW), IS TO MAKE THE DOUGH BALLS THE PERFECT SIZE. IF THERE ARE KIDS AROUND TO HELP, THEY LOVE THIS TASK. IF NOT, BE PATIENT AND DO IT RIGHT. IT'S WORTH IT. OH, DON'T GET SCARED OFF BY THE YEAST. IT'S NOT THAT KIND OF BATTER!

CAKE
1 cup sour cream
2 1/4-ounce packages active dry yeast
4 tablespoons granulated sugar
4 large eggs, room temperature
1/2 pound (2 sticks) unsalted butter, melted and cooled
5 cups all-purpose flour
1 teaspoon baking powder
1/2 teaspoon salt

Preheat the oven to 350 degrees. Grease and flour a 10-inch tube pan. Set aside.

Mix the sour cream with the yeast and let sit for 5 minutes. Using an electric mixer on medium speed, add the sugar to the yeast mixture and combine well. Add eggs, one at a time, mixing well after each addition. In a medium bowl, combine flour, baking powder, and salt and add to the batter alternately with the melted butter, working with your hands to combine well. Do not overmix at this point. Chill the batter for 1 hour or more.

FILLING
1/4 pound (1 stick) unsalted butter
1 1/2 cups granulated sugar
2 tablespoons ground cinnamon
1/2 cup finely chopped pecan pieces

In a small saucepan, melt the butter. Pour into a small bowl. Combine sugar, cinnamon, and chopped nuts in another small bowl.

Remove the batter from the refrigerator. Pinch off the dough in small amounts (large marble size) and roll into balls. (Don't let these balls get too big as the process goes on. Remember: little is good!) Dip each ball into the melted butter. Then, coat each ball well in the sugar mixture. Layer the balls in the tube pan until you have used them all, occasionally sprinkling some of the filling between each layer. Sprinkle any remaining sugar mixture over the top layer.

Bake on center rack in oven for about 55 minutes or until a cake tester comes out clean. Let the cake cool completely on a wire rack before turning it out of the pan.

Store the cake at room temperature.

Serves 12—14.

Note: You can easily slice this cake. However, for some strange reason, people take great pleasure in simply "pulling it apart," ball by ball. Not the most delicate approach, but obviously a most satisfying one.

Muffins

We think the reason people gravitate toward muffins is because it gives them an excuse to eat dessert any time of the day. After all, many muffins are simply cake-type batters baked in muffin tins. If you are into sweet muffins, don't stop here. Try our Chocolate Chocolate Cake or Quaker Oatmeal Cake made as muffins. After you've made that leap, you might refer to them as cupcakes.

We use large muffin tins. But feel free to vary the size of your muffins depending on your needs. A medium-size muffin is the perfect addition to a brown-bag lunch. "Itty bitty" muffins are a delightful addition to any brunch/dessert buffet.

Our offerings here range from A to Z, but no matter its size, no matter its flavor, sometimes "muffin else will do."

RECIPES

CRANBERRY GINGER MUFFINS

*I*N THE FALL, WHEN CRANBERRIES ARE ABUNDANT, TRY THESE MUFFINS. HEAT THEM. THEY MAKE A COMFORTING SNACK ON A CHILLY AFTERNOON.

6 ounces (1 1/2 sticks) unsalted butter,
   room temperature
3/4 cup dark brown sugar, packed
2 large eggs, room temperature
1 teaspoon vanilla extract
4 cups all-purpose flour
1 1/2 teaspoons ground cinnamon
1 1/2 teaspoons ground ginger
1/4 teaspoon ground cloves

3/4 teaspoon ground allspice
2 teaspoons baking soda
2 teaspoons baking powder
1/4 teaspoon salt
3/4 cup molasses
1 1/8 cups buttermilk
1/3 cup crystallized ginger, chopped
2 1/4 cups fresh cranberries, coarsely chopped

Preheat the oven to 350 degrees. Line a muffin tin with paper muffin cups. Set aside.

Using an electric mixer on medium speed, cream butter. Add brown sugar and beat until fluffy. Add eggs, one at a time, and vanilla extract and continue mixing until well blended, about 5 minutes. In a medium bowl, combine the dry ingredients, and add slowly to the mixture. Using a rubber spatula, scrape down the sides of the mixing bowl. Add molasses and buttermilk and mix well. Scrape down the sides of the bowl again. On low speed, stir in chopped ginger and the cranberries. Mix well but do not overbeat.

Pour the batter to the top of the muffin cups and bake on center rack in oven for 25–30 minutes or until a cake tester comes out clean.

Cool on a wire rack before removing muffins from tin.

Store the muffins at room temperature.

Yields 18–20 large muffins.

APPLE NUT MUFFINS

*U*SE THE APPLE OF YOUR CHOICE TO MAKE THESE MUFFINS. WE LOVE THE TART GRANNY SMITHS. SINCE APPLES ARE ALWAYS AVAILABLE, THESE MOIST MUFFINS ARE GREAT YEAR-ROUND.

BATTER
1 1/2 cups light brown sugar, packed
2/3 cup vegetable oil
1 large egg, room temperature
1 teaspoon vanilla extract
2 1/2 cups all-purpose flour

1 teaspoon baking soda
1 teaspoon salt
1 cup buttermilk
1 1/2 cups peeled and diced apples
1 cup pecan pieces

Preheat the oven to 350 degrees. Line a muffin tin with paper muffin cups. Set aside.

Using an electric mixer on medium speed, combine brown sugar, oil, egg, and vanilla extract and beat until the mixture thickens. In a small bowl, combine flour, baking soda, and salt. Add the dry ingredients to the liquid mixture alternately with buttermilk. Mix gently, using a rubber spatula to scrape down the sides of the bowl. DO NOT OVERMIX! Stir in apples and pecan pieces.

Pour the batter to the top of the muffin cups. Sprinkle lightly with the topping.

TOPPING
1/3 cup granulated sugar
1 teaspoon unsalted butter, melted and cooled

In a small saucepan over low heat, melt the butter. In a small bowl, combine the sugar and melted butter. Sprinkle the mixture over the tops of the muffins and bake on center rack in oven for 25–30 minutes or until a cake tester comes out clean.

Cool on a wire rack before removing from tin.

Store the muffins at room temperature.

Yields 12–14 large muffins.

MORNING GLORY MUFFINS

WE'VE ALWAYS HEARD THESE REFERRED TO AS MORNING GLORY MUFFINS. AT THE MODICA MARKET IN SEASIDE, FLORIDA, THEY ARE CALLED GLORIOUS MORNINGS. WE WISH WE HAD THOUGHT OF THAT NAME FIRST.

1 1/3 cups granulated sugar
2 1/8 cups all-purpose flour
1 tablespoon ground cinnamon
2 teaspoons baking soda
1/2 teaspoon salt
1/2 cup sweetened coconut
1/2 cup raisins
2 cups peeled and grated carrots (approximately 4 medium carrots)
1 medium apple, finely chopped
1 20-ounce can crushed pineapple, well drained
1/2 cup pecan pieces
3 large eggs, room temperature
1 cup vegetable oil
1 teaspoon vanilla extract

Preheat the oven to 350 degrees. Line a muffin tin with paper muffin cups. Set aside.

Using an electric mixer on low speed, combine sugar, flour, cinnamon, baking soda, and salt. Add coconut, raisins, carrots, apples, drained pineapple, and pecans. Mix well. Using a rubber spatula, scrape down the sides of the bowl. In a small bowl, combine eggs, oil, and vanilla extract. On low speed, add the egg mixture to the batter and blend well.

Fill each muffin cup to the top and bake on center rack in oven for approximately 30 minutes or until a cake tester comes out clean.

Cool on a wire rack before removing from tin.

Store the muffins at room temperature.

Yields 16 large muffins.

Pumpkin Raisin Spice Muffins

Years ago, we developed this recipe as a seasonal offering. These moist, spicy muffins became so popular that The Dessert Place now serves them throughout the year. They are a special treat on Halloween morning (or any morning)!

1 cup raisins
1/2 cup hot water
2 large eggs, room temperature
1 1/3 cups granulated sugar
1 cup pumpkin (yes, canned is OK!)
1 teaspoon vanilla extract
3/4 cup vegetable oil
1 2/3 cups all-purpose flour
1 teaspoon ground cinnamon
1 teaspoon ground cloves
1 1/2 teaspoons baking powder
1 1/2 teaspoons baking soda
3/4 teaspoon salt

Preheat the oven to 350 degrees. Line a muffin tin with paper muffin cups. Set aside.

In a small bowl, combine raisins and water and set aside. Using an electric mixer on medium speed, beat eggs. Add sugar and continue to beat until the mixture thickens. Blend in pumpkin and vanilla extract. Pour in oil and continue mixing. Scrape down the sides of the bowl with a rubber spatula and add raisins and water, mixing well. In a small bowl, combine flour, spices, baking powder, baking soda, and salt. Add to the batter and mix on low speed until just blended. Do not overbeat.

Fill the muffin cups to the top and bake on the center rack in oven for approximately 30 minutes or until a cake tester comes out clean.

Cool on a wire rack before removing from tin.

Store the muffins at room temperature.

Yields 12 large muffins.

BLUEBERRY MUFFINS

*I*T TOOK US FOREVER TO DEVELOP THE PERFECT BLUEBERRY MUFFIN. WHEN SHEA MEDDIN (SHERYL'S SON) FINALLY GAVE HIS APPROVAL, WE KNEW WE HAD IT RIGHT.

> 1 3/4 cups fresh blueberries
> 2 cups all-purpose flour
> 1 tablespoon baking powder
> 1/2 teaspoon salt
> 1 cup granulated sugar
> 1 large egg, room temperature
> 1 cup milk
> 1/8 pound (1/2 stick) unsalted butter, melted

Preheat the oven to 350 degrees. Line a muffin tin with paper muffin cups. Set aside.

In a small bowl, combine blueberries with 1/4 cup flour and set aside. Using an electric mixer on low speed, combine the remaining 1 3/4 cups flour with baking powder, salt and 3/4 cup sugar. Add egg. Using a rubber spatula, scrape down the sides of the bowl and add milk and melted butter. Do not overbeat. Gently stir in the blueberry/flour mixture. (This batter should not be smooth!)

Pour the batter to the top of the muffin cups. Using the remaining 1/4 cup sugar, sprinkle the top of each muffin with approximately 1 teaspoon of sugar.

Bake on center rack in oven for 25–30 minutes or until a cake tester comes out clean. Cool on a wire rack before removing from tin.

Store the muffins at room temperature.

Yields 8–10 large muffins.

ℒUCCHINI MUFFINS

ALTHOUGH THEY ARE CLEARLY NOT A HEALTH-FOOD ITEM, TRISH KOLBER (SHERYL'S SISTER) JUSTIFIES EATING THESE MUFFINS BECAUSE OF THEIR VEGGIE CONTENT. WHO IS SHE KIDDING?

- 3 *large eggs, room temperature*
- 1 1/4 *cups vegetable oil*
- 1 1/2 *cups granulated sugar*
- 1 *teaspoon vanilla extract*
- 1 1/2 *cups grated zucchini*
- 2 *cups all-purpose flour*
- 2 *teaspoons baking soda*
- 1 *teaspoon baking powder*
- 1 *teaspoon salt*
- 1 *teaspoon ground cinnamon*
- 1 *teaspoon ground cloves*
- 1 *cup chopped walnuts*

Preheat the oven to 350 degrees. Line a muffin tin with paper muffin cups. Set aside.

Using an electric mixer on medium speed, beat eggs, oil, sugar, and vanilla extract until light and thickened. Stir in grated zucchini. In a small bowl, combine the dry ingredients and add to the mixture. Scrape down the sides of the bowl with a rubber spatula and, on low speed, stir in walnuts. Do not overbeat.

Pour the batter to the top of the muffin cups and bake on center rack in oven for 25–30 minutes or until a cake tester comes out clean.

Cool on a wire rack before removing from tin.

Store the muffins at room temperature.

Yields 12–14 large muffins.

$\mathcal{P}$IES

THE AROMA OF PIES BAKING IN THE OVEN CONJURES UP CHILDHOOD MEMORIES (OR, FOR THE LESS FORTUNATE, CHILDHOOD FANTASIES). PERHAPS PIES ARE SO PLENTIFUL BECAUSE THEY ARE SO EASY TO MAKE. THAT EXPRESSION "EASY AS PIE" HAD TO COME FROM SOMEWHERE!

THE ONE THING THAT SCARES A LOT OF PEOPLE AWAY FROM MAKING PIES IS THE COMMON "FEAR OF CRUSTS." THERE IS NO REASON FOR THIS. THE PIE-CRUST RECIPE WE'VE INCLUDED IS EASY AND GRATIFYING. REALLY! SO, FORGE AHEAD. IF YOU'RE STILL NOT CONVINCED, THERE IS AN ALTERNATIVE. DON'T SAY WE EVER SAID THIS, BUT YOU COULD BE SNEAKY ABOUT IT AND RESORT TO A STORE-BOUGHT FROZEN CRUST. DEFROST AND TRANSFER THE CRUST TO YOUR OWN PIE PLATE. THE RESULTS WON'T BE QUITE AS REWARDING (OR DELICIOUS), BUT AT LEAST YOU WILL HAVE DEALT WITH YOUR FEARS.

ON TO THE FILLINGS. NO EXCUSES HERE. PIE FILLINGS ARE INCREDIBLY SIMPLE TO CONCOCT. THE ONES WE'VE INCLUDED RANGE FROM THE WICKEDLY RICH TO THE DELIGHTFULLY TART, EACH ONE SERVING 6–8 GUESTS, AND EACH ONE "AS EASY AS PIE."

RECIPES

APPLE PIE

USE GRANNY SMITHS FOR A TART, CRUNCHIER PIE, OR USE ROME BEAUTIES FOR A SWEETER, SOFTER RESULT. EITHER WAY, THIS IS THE GREAT APPLE PIE YOU WISH YOUR MOTHER HAD MADE!

CRUST
1 1/2 cups all-purpose flour
1/2 teaspoon ground cinnamon
1/4 pound (1 stick) unsalted butter, very cold and cut into 1/2-inch pieces
1/4 cup apple juice, very cold

In a food processor fitted with a metal blade, process flour and cinnamon until blended. Add butter to the machine all at once. "Pulse" on and off 4–6 times until the mixture resembles coarse meal. With the machine running, add cold apple juice. Process just until the dough begins to form a ball. DO NOT OVERPROCESS.

Gather the dough into a ball with your hands and flatten it into an 8-inch disc. Wrap the disc in waxed paper and refrigerate at least 8 hours before handling. (The dough may also be frozen at this point and kept for later use. If frozen, defrost the dough for 12 hours in the refrigerator before using.) Remove the dough from the refrigerator 20–30 minutes before rolling.

Preheat the oven to 350 degrees.

Sprinkle flour over a flat surface and with a floured rolling pin roll the disc into a 15-inch circle. Transfer carefully into a 9-inch deep-dish pie pan. Trim the dough, leaving enough to allow for shrinkage and to finish the edge decoratively. Prick the crust with a fork several times before baking.

Bake the crust on the center rack in oven for 12–15 minutes or until lightly golden. Let the crust cool completely before filling.

FILLING
6 medium apples
2/3 cup sour cream
1/4 cup all-purpose flour
1 large egg, room temperature
1/2 cup granulated sugar
1/2 teaspoon salt
1/2 teaspoon vanilla extract
1/2 teaspoon ground cinnamon

Peel, core, and slice apples. In a large bowl, combine the remaining ingredients. Toss apples into the filling using only enough to coat them lightly. Pile the flavored apples into the cooked crust and then spread the topping over the fruit.

TOPPING
2/3 cup all-purpose flour
1/4 cup light brown sugar, packed
1/8 cup granulated sugar
1/2 teaspoon ground cinnamon
1/4 cup pecan pieces
1/8 teaspoon salt
6 tablespoons (3/4 stick) unsalted butter, cold and cut into 1/2-inch pieces

In a food processor fitted with a metal blade, combine all of the ingredients except butter. Add butter to the flour mixture all at once. Pulse until the mixture resembles coarse meal.

Distribute the topping over apples, completely covering the pie. Bake for 1–1 1/4 hours, until the topping is a golden brown. Let the pie cool completely on a wire rack before cutting.

If baking in advance, refrigerate the pie but bring it to room temperature or heat before serving.

Serves 6–8.

Note: On a hot summer day, this apple pie calls out for the ubiquitous scoop of ice cream. But, for a day when there's that nip in the air, try it heated with a slice of sharp cheddar cheese.

KEY LIME PIE

*T*ART, CREAMY, SUMMERY, REFRESHING. A TASTE OF THE FLORIDA KEYS WHEREVER YOU ARE!

CRUST
1 1/2 cups graham cracker crumbs
3 tablespoons granulated sugar
1/8 pound (1/2 stick) unsalted butter, melted

Preheat the oven to 325 degrees.

In a medium bowl, combine graham cracker crumbs and sugar. Add melted butter and mix until well blended. Using your fingertips, press into a 9-inch deep-dish pie pan. Set aside.

Bake the crust on center rack in oven for approximately 10 minutes, or until lightly browned. Let the crust cool completely before filling.

FILLING
1 1/4 pounds cream cheese, room temperature
3/4 cup Key lime juice
1/2 teaspoon vanilla extract
1 small can (14 ounces) sweetened condensed milk

Using an electric mixer on medium speed, beat the cream cheese until soft. Do not whip. Continuing to mix on medium speed, add Key lime juice, vanilla extract, and condensed milk. Mix just until well blended.

Pour the filling into the baked, cooled graham cracker crust and refrigerate the pie until set, at least 8 hours or overnight.

Refrigerate the pie until ready to serve.

Serves 6—8.

Note: This pie also tastes great with the chocolate crumb crust like the one we use for the Lemon Light Pie (page 67), and Sweetened Whipped Cream Frosting (page 16) is always an option.

Crack eggs, individually, into a separate bowl before adding them to a batter. This way, you can avoid any "bad eggs" that might be lurking and also ensure no shells get by you.

MARM'S PEANUT BUTTER PIE

*T*HERE IS NOTHING LIGHT ABOUT THIS PIE. THE PEANUT BUTTER COOKIE CRUST AND PEANUT BUTTER CHOCOLATE FILLING ARE RICH, BUTTERY, AND SINFUL. GO FOR IT!

CRUST

1/4 pound (1 stick) unsalted butter, room temperature
1/2 cup peanut butter, crunchy or creamy
1/2 cup granulated sugar
1/2 cup light brown sugar, packed
1 large egg, room temperature
1/2 teaspoon vanilla extract
1 cup all-purpose flour
1/4 teaspoon baking soda
1/4 teaspoon baking powder
1/4 teaspoon salt
1/4 cup milk

Preheat the oven to 325 degrees. Grease a 9-inch deep-dish pie pan. Set aside.

Using an electric mixer on medium speed, cream together butter and peanut butter. Add sugars and beat on medium speed until thoroughly combined. Add egg and vanilla extract and continue mixing. Scrape down the sides of the bowl with a rubber spatula and beat until light and fluffy, about 5 minutes. In a small bowl, combine flour, baking soda, baking powder and salt, and slowly add to the batter on low speed. Mix until well combined. Add milk and mix well. Using your fingertips, press the batter into bottom and up the sides of the pie pan, covering the rim.

Bake on center rack in oven for 15–25 minutes or until lightly browned. Let the crust cool completely before filling.

FILLING

1/2 pound (2 sticks) unsalted butter, room temperature
2 cups confectioners' sugar
1 teaspoon vanilla extract
3/4 cup semi-sweet chocolate, melted
1/2 cup peanut butter, crunchy or creamy

Using an electric mixer on medium speed, cream the butter. Add confectioners' sugar and vanilla extract and mix until light and fluffy, about 5 minutes. Divide the batter equally into two small bowls. To one half of the batter, stir in the melted chocolate. To the other half, stir in the peanut butter.

Spread the chocolate mixture into the crust. Then evenly distribute the peanut butter mixture on top. Using the end of a wooden spoon, gently swirl the two mixtures to blend them together, but do not mix them thoroughly. Because you want to have two distinct flavors and colors, the fillings should look "marbleized." Refrigerate the pie for at least 1 hour before topping with the Overkill Chocolate Glaze.

OVERKILL CHOCOLATE GLAZE

1 cup semi-sweet chocolate chips
1–2 tablespoons cognac

In a small saucepan over very low heat, melt chocolate chips and add cognac. Stir until smooth. Drizzle over the top of the pie.

Refrigerate the pie but bring it to room temperature before serving.

Serves 8–10.

TRIO PIE

Chocolate Cookie Crust ...Chocolate Mousse Filling ...Chocolate Whipped Cream ...

CRUST
3/4 cup all-purpose flour
5 tablespoons light brown sugar, packed
1/2 teaspoon salt
1/8 pound (1/2 stick) unsalted butter, cold
1/2 cup pecan pieces
1 ounce unsweetened chocolate, coarsely grated and chilled
2 tablespoons cold water

Preheat the oven to 325 degrees. Grease a 9-inch deep dish pie pan. Set aside.

Using an electric mixer on low speed, combine flour, sugar and salt. Cut butter into small chunks and add it, along with pecan pieces and grated chocolate, to the dry ingredients. Mix until blended. Add just enough water to hold the crust firmly together. Using your fingertips, press the batter into the bottom and up the sides of the pie pan, covering the rim.

Bake on center rack in oven for approximately 20 minutes, until lightly browned. Let the crust cool completely before filling.

FILLING
6 ounces (1 1/2 sticks) unsalted butter, room temperature
1 1/4 cups confectioners' sugar
3 large eggs, room temperature
2 ounces unsweetened chocolate, melted and cooled
1 teaspoon vanilla extract
1 teaspoon instant coffee powder
1/2 teaspoon salt

Using an electric mixer on medium speed, cream butter. Add sugar, scraping down the sides of the bowl with a rubber spatula, and beat until the mixture is light and fluffy, about 5 minutes.

Add the eggs, one at a time, mixing for 1 minute after each addition. In a small bowl, combine unsweetened chocolate with vanilla extract, instant coffee powder, and salt. Add this to the butter/sugar mixture and beat well for several minutes. Scrape down the bowl again and mix for 1 more minute.

Pour the filling into the cooled crust and chill the pie for at least 4 hours before topping with the whipped cream.

TOPPING
1 cup heavy cream, chilled
2 tablespoon confectioners' sugar
2 teaspoons cocoa (or to taste)
Chocolate shavings (for garnish)

Before serving, whip the cream with the sugar with an electric mixer on high speed until the mixture begins to thicken. Add the cocoa and beat the cream until stiff. Be careful not to overbeat cream or it will turn into butter. Spread the whipped cream over the top of the chocolate filling. Garnish the pie with chocolate shavings, if desired.

Refrigerate the pie but bring it to room temperature before serving.

Serves 6–8.

PECAN PIE

WE GUESS IF YOU'RE A SOUTHERN BOY LIKE TOM WHITE (OUR FRIEND CALLIE'S/CAROLINE'S HUSBAND) OF SPARTANBURG, SOUTH CAROLINA, PECAN PIE RANKS RIGHT UP THERE. TOMMY-DOO, THIS PIE'S FOR YOU.

CRUST
1/2 recipe Basic Flaky Pie Crust (page 69), unbaked

Follow directions for Basic Flaky Pie Crust, using a 9-inch deep dish pie pan. Refrigerate the unbaked crust until ready to use.

FILLING
4 large eggs, room temperature
1 cup dark brown sugar
3/4 cup light corn syrup
1/8 pound (1/2 stick) unsalted butter, melted and cooled

2 teaspoons vanilla extract
3/4 teaspoon salt
2 cups pecan pieces
1/2 cup pecan halves

Preheat the oven to 350 degrees.

Using an electric mixer on medium speed, beat eggs until frothy. Add brown sugar and corn syrup and continue mixing until well blended. Scrape down the sides of the bowl with a rubber spatula and add the melted butter, vanilla extract, and salt. Mix thoroughly.

Sprinkle the pecan pieces into the bottom of the unbaked pie crust. Pour the filling over the pecans. Place the pecan halves around the rim of the pie in a decorative fashion. Bake on center rack in oven for 45–55 minutes or until the center of the filling is set.

Cool completely on a wire rack.

Store the pie at room temperature.

Serves 6–8.

Note: Serve this pie heated with ice cream and/or fresh whipped cream.

KENTUCKY PIE

*P*ECANS AND JACK DANIEL'S BOURBON MAKE THIS A SOUTHERN STAPLE. THE CHOCOLATE CHIPS MAKE IT A FAVORITE.

CRUST
1/2 recipe Basic Flaky Pie Crust (page 69), unbaked

Follow directions for Basic Flaky Pie Crust using a 9-inch deep-dish pie pan. Refrigerate the unbaked crust until ready to use.

FILLING
2 large eggs, room temperature
1 cup granulated sugar
1/2 teaspoon salt
1/2 cup all-purpose flour
1/4 pound (1 stick) unsalted butter, melted and cooled
1 1/2 tablespoons Jack Daniel's bourbon
1 teaspoon vanilla extract
3/4 cup chocolate chips
1 cup pecan pieces

Preheat the oven to 350 degrees.

Using an electric mixer on high speed, beat eggs until light and pale yellow in color. Gradually add sugar and salt. On low speed, add flour and melted butter and mix thoroughly until well blended. Using a rubber spatula, scrape down the sides and bottom of the bowl, and add bourbon and vanilla extract. Stir in chocolate chips and pecan pieces.

Pour the filling into the unbaked pie crust. Bake on center rack in oven for 40 minutes or until golden brown. Cool completely on a wire rack.

Store the pie at room temperature.

Serves 6—8.

Note: This pie is delicious served heated with fresh whipped cream or ice cream.

VERY BERRY PIE

*B*UY WHATEVER BERRIES STRIKE YOUR FANCY. THE MORE THE BERRIER!

CRUST
1/2 recipe Basic Flaky Pie Crust (page 69) (if using the crumb topping)
OR 1 recipe Basic Flaky Pie Crust (if making a lattice or solid top crust)

Follow directions for Basic Flaky Pie Crust using a 9-inch deep-dish pie pan. Refrigerate the unbaked crust until ready to use.

Preheat the oven to 350 degrees. Bake pie crust on center rack in oven for approximately 10 minutes or until slightly brown. Let the crust cool completely before filling.

FILLING
1 tablespoon cornstarch
1 tablespoon lemon juice
1 cup granulated sugar
3 cups fresh assorted berries
3 cups sliced strawberries

In a large bowl, blend cornstarch and lemon juice until smooth. Add sugar and mix until blended. Toss fruit into the cornstarch/sugar mixture and let the mixture sit for 15–20 minutes. Toss again and drain off the excess liquid.

Pour the fruit mixture into the baked pie crust. Top with the crumb topping mixture or with a lattice or solid top crust.

CRUMB TOPPING
2/3 cup all-purpose flour
1/3 cup granulated sugar
1/3 cup light brown sugar, packed
1/8 pound (1/2 stick) unsalted butter, cold

Using an electric mixer on low speed, combine flour and sugars. Cut butter into 1/2-inch pieces and add to the flour/sugar mixture. Mix until it resembles coarse meal. Sprinkle crumb topping over the fruit.

Bake the pie on center rack in oven for 1–1 1/4 hours or until the crust or topping is golden brown. Cool completely on a wire rack.

If pie is made in advance, refrigerate the pie but bring it to room temperature or heat before serving.

Serves 6–8.

STRAWBERRY RHUBARB PIE

You MIGHT NOT EVEN KNOW YOU LIKE RHUBARB UNTIL YOU'VE TASTED THIS PIE.

CRUST
1/2 recipe Basic Flaky Pie Crust (page 69) (if using the crumb topping)
OR 1 recipe Basic Pie Crust (if making a lattice or solid top crust)

Follow directions for Basic Flaky Pie Crust using a 9-inch deep-dish pie pan. Refrigerate the unbaked crust until ready to use.

Preheat the oven to 350 degrees. Bake the pie crust on center rack in oven for approximately 10 minutes or until golden brown. Let the crust cool completely before filling.

FILLING
1 tablespoon cornstarch
1 tablespoon lime juice
1 cup granulated sugar
3 cups rhubarb, sliced in 1/2-inch pieces
3 cups sliced strawberries

Using an electric mixer on low speed, blend the cornstarch and lime juice until smooth. Add the sugar to the cornstarch mixture and mix well on medium speed. Toss the fruit in the cornstarch/sugar mixture. Let the mixture sit for 15–20 minutes. Toss well again and drain off the excess liquid.

Pour the fruit mixture into the baked pie crust. Top with either a lattice or solid top crust or a crumb topping. (For crumb topping, see Very Berry Pie, page 64). Bake the pie on center rack in oven for 1–1 1/4 hours or until the crust or topping is golden brown.

Cool completely on a wire rack.

If pie is made in advance, refrigerate the pie but bring it to room temperature or heat before serving.

Serves 6–8.

ℒEMON LIGHT PIE

*T*HIS LEMON-CHOCOLATE COMBINATION IS A DELIGHTFUL SURPRISE. MAKE THE CRUST AS THICK AS YOU LIKE. IT WON'T DETRACT FROM THE LIGHT CITRUS FILLING.

CRUST
9-ounce package chocolate wafers
1/8 pound (1/2 stick) unsalted butter, melted

Preheat the oven to 350 degrees. Use a 9-inch deep-dish pie pan.

In a food processor fitted with a metal blade, process chocolate wafers until finely ground. Add melted butter and blend well. Using your fingertips, press the chocolate crumb mixture into the pie pan.

Bake the crust on center rack in oven for 7–8 minutes and let cool completely before filling.

FILLING
3 large eggs, separated, room temperature   *Rind of 1 large lemon, grated*
1 can (14 ounces) condensed milk   *1/4 teaspoon cream of tartar*
1/2 cup lemon juice   *1/2 cup granulated sugar*

In a medium bowl, using a hand-held electric mixer on medium speed, combine egg yolks, condensed milk, lemon juice, and grated lemon rind. Using an electric stand mixer, beat the egg whites on medium speed until frothy and add cream of tartar. Beating on high speed, slowly add sugar and beat until stiff peaks form. Gently, fold yolk mixture into beaten egg whites.

Pour the batter into the baked, cooled crust. Bake on center rack in oven for 12–15 minutes or until the top begins to turn golden. Allow the pie to cool completely on a wire rack. Refrigerate the pie for at least 4 hours or overnight.

Refrigerate the pie until ready to serve.

Serves 6–8.

Note: To make a Lime Light Pie, simply substitute limes for the lemons.

You know what they say about rules and exceptions. When making pie crust, you want the butter, shortening, and liquid as cold as possible!

BASIC FLAKY PIE CRUST

*E*VERYONE HAS A FAVORITE PIE CRUST RECIPE. THIS ONE, COURTESY OF ELLEN BAKST (SHERYL'S MOM), IS OURS. THIS DOUGH MAY SEEM DIFFICULT TO HANDLE, BUT IT IS WORTH THE EFFORT. BE PATIENT. IT MAKES A GREAT FLAKY CRUST. THIS RECIPE MAKES ENOUGH DOUGH FOR EITHER TWO 9-INCH DEEP-DISH BOTTOM CRUSTS OR ONE BOTTOM AND ONE TOP (SOLID OR LATTICE) CRUST.

2 1/2 cups all-purpose flour
1/2 teaspoon salt
1/4 pound (1 stick) unsalted butter,
    very cold and cut into 1/2-inch pieces

1 tablespoon granulated sugar
1/4 cup butter-flavored vegetable shortening
4—5 tablespoons ice water

Using a food processor fitted with a metal blade, combine flour, salt, and sugar. Add butter and shortening all at once, and "pulse" the processor on and off until the mixture resembles coarse meal. With the machine running, add ice water 1 tablespoon at a time until the mixture begins to hold together. (Stop processing before the dough forms a ball.)

Gather the dough into a ball with your hands and divide in half. Flatten each half into an 8-inch disc and wrap in waxed paper. Refrigerate at least 8 hours before handling. (The dough may also be frozen at this point and kept for later use. If frozen, defrost the dough in the refrigerator before using.) Remove the dough from the refrigerator 20–30 minutes before rolling.

Preheat the oven to 350 degrees.

Sprinkle a flat surface with flour and, using a floured rolling pin, roll out one disc into a 15-inch circle. Carefully transfer the dough into the 9-inch deep-dish pie pan. Trim the dough, leaving enough to allow for shrinkage and to finish the edge decoratively. Prick the crust with a fork several times before baking.

Bake on center rack in oven for 15–20 minutes or until lightly browned.

Cool the crust completely.

Note: If you are using either a lattice or solid top crust, lightly brush the dough, before baking, with a mixture of 1 egg beaten with 1 tablespoon water. You might also want to lightly sprinkle the crust with granulated sugar. If you opt for the solid top crust, don't forget to make several slits in the top before baking the pie.

Cookies

OOKIES AREN'T JUST FOR KIDS. ALTHOUGH WE'VE INCLUDED SEVERAL OF THEIR FAVORITES (CHOCOLATE CHIP AND OATMEAL RAISIN), MOST OF THESE COOKIES ARE SOPHISTICATED ENOUGH TO BE SERVED TO YOUR MOST DISTINGUISHED COLLEAGUES.

IN EACH OF THESE RECIPES, WE HAVE STATED THE APPROXIMATE YIELD. BUT THESE NUMBERS ARE IN YOUR CONTROL. IF YOU ARE MAKING A "BIRTHDAY COOKIE," SUDDENLY A RECIPE FOR TWO DOZEN COOKIES MAKES ONLY ONE COOKIE CAKE. AND FOR A HOUSE FULL OF MUNCHERS, A COOKIE THE SIZE OF A QUARTER MAY BE THE ANSWER TO YOUR SNACKING PROBLEMS. SO USE THESE COOKIE RECIPES TO SUIT YOUR OWN NEEDS.

AS IF COOKIES WEREN'T ALREADY A BREEZE TO MAKE, YOU CAN FURTHER SIMPLIFY THE PROCESS BY EITHER REFRIGERATING (OR FREEZING) THE BATTER FOR A WEEK (OR A MONTH). AFTER YOU BRING THE BATTER TO ROOM TEMPERATURE, THE RESULTS ARE THE SAME: FRESH BAKED COOKIES ANY TIME, ANY DAY!

RECIPES

CHOCOLATE CHIP COOKIES

*D*ON'T OVERBAKE THESE. THEY'RE SUPPOSED TO BE SOFT AND CHEWY IN THE CENTER, JUST THE WAY MARISA MEDDIN (SHERYL'S DAUGHTER) LOVES THEM!

> 1/2 pound (2 sticks) unsalted butter, room temperature
> 3/4 cup granulated sugar
> 3/4 cup light brown sugar, packed
> 2 large eggs, room temperature
> 2 teaspoons vanilla extract
> 2 1/2 cups all-purpose flour
> 1 1/4 teaspoons baking soda
> 1 teaspoon salt
> 2 cups semi-sweet chocolate chips
> 1 cup pecan pieces (optional)

Preheat the oven to 350 degrees. Line a baking sheet with parchment paper or grease the sheet well. Set aside.

Using an electric mixer on medium speed, cream butter. Add both sugars and mix well. Add eggs, one at a time, and vanilla extract, all the while scraping down the sides of the bowl with a rubber spatula. Continue mixing until the batter is light and fluffy, approximately 5 minutes. In a small bowl, combine flour, baking soda, and salt and add to the batter. Scrape down the sides of the bowl again and mix until blended. On low speed, stir in the chocolate chips (and the pecans, if you are using them).

Scoop rounded tablespoons of the dough onto the baking sheet, about 2 inches apart.

Bake on center rack in oven for 15–17 minutes or until golden brown. Cool on a wire rack.

Store the cookies in an airtight container.

Yields approximately 36 cookies.

OATMEAL RAISIN COOKIES

◡

*P*EOPLE SEEM TO BE VERY PARTICULAR ABOUT THEIR OATMEAL RAISIN COOKIES. ONE GROUP LIKES THEM THIN AND CHEWY. ANOTHER GROUP LIKES THEM THICK AND CRUNCHY. WE THINK WE STRUCK A BEAUTIFUL BALANCE HERE. THESE COOKIES ARE THICK AND CHEWY. BE CAREFUL NOT TO OVER BAKE THEM.

6 ounces (1 1/2 sticks) unsalted butter, room temperature
1/4 cup plus 1 tablespoon vegetable shortening
3/4 cup granulated sugar
3/4 cup light brown sugar, packed
1 large egg, room temperature
1 teaspoon vanilla extract
1 1/2 cups all-purpose flour
1 teaspoon baking soda
1 teaspoon ground cinnamon
3/4 teaspoon salt
2 cups Quaker quick oats
1 1/4 cups raisins

Preheat the oven to 350 degrees. Line a baking sheet with parchment paper or grease the sheet well. Set aside.

Using an electric mixer on medium speed, cream butter and shortening. Add sugars and continue beating until light and fluffy, about 5 minutes. Add egg and vanilla extract, scrape down the sides of the bowl with a rubber spatula, and continue beating until the egg is well blended. In a small bowl, combine flour, baking soda, cinnamon, and salt, and add it slowly to the mixing bowl. Scrape down the bowl again, and add oats. Blend well. Stir in raisins.

Scoop rounded tablespoons of the dough onto the baking sheet, about 2 inches apart.

Bake on center rack in oven for approximately 13–14 minutes, or until very lightly browned. Cool on a wire rack.

Store the cookies in an airtight container.

Yields approximately 3 dozen cookies.

CHOCOLATE FUDGE CHEWIES

*I*T'S AMAZING. NO EGG YOLKS, NO BUTTER, NO OIL, NO SHORTENING. AND STILL THESE COOKIES ARE ABSOLUTELY FABULOUS. MICHAEL BURTON (BENNETT'S BEAU) SWEARS HE IS ADDICTED TO THESE.

> 3 cups confectioners' sugar
> 1/2 cup plus 2 tablespoons cocoa
> 2 tablespoons all-purpose flour
> 1 teaspoon salt
> 3 large egg whites, room temperature
> 1 teaspoon vanilla extract
> 2 cups pecan pieces

Preheat the oven to 350 degrees. Line a baking sheet with parchment paper or grease the sheet well. Set aside.

Using an electric mixer on medium speed, combine sugar, cocoa, flour, and salt and mix until well blended. Beat in egg whites, one at a time, scraping down the bowl with a rubber spatula after each addition. Add vanilla extract and beat at high speed for 1 minute. Stir in pecan pieces.

Scoop rounded tablespoons of the dough onto the baking sheet, about 2 inches apart.

Bake on center rack in oven 12–15 minutes or until the cookies just begin to crack on top. Cool on a wire rack.

Store the cookies in an airtight container.

Yields approximately 2 dozen cookies.

PEANUT BUTTER COOKIES

EANUT BUTTER PURISTS PREFER THESE PLAIN. THE MORE ADVENTURESOME MIGHT PREFER THEM WITH THEIR CHOCOLATE GLAZE. IT'S A TOSS-UP. THEY ARE DELICIOUS EITHER WAY.

DOUGH

1/4 pound (1 stick) unsalted butter
1/2 cup light brown sugar, packed
1/2 cup granulated sugar
1 large egg, room temperature
1/2 teaspoon vanilla extract

1 cup chunky peanut butter
1 1/3 cups all-purpose flour
1/2 teaspoon salt
1/2 teaspoon baking soda

Preheat the oven to 350 degrees. Line a baking sheet with parchment paper or grease the sheet well. Set aside.

Using an electric mixer on medium speed, cream butter. Add sugars and mix until the batter is light and fluffy, about 5 minutes. Add egg and beat until the batter is light and fluffy again, scraping down the sides of the bowl with a rubber spatula as needed. Add vanilla extract and peanut butter and mix well. In a small bowl, combine flour, salt, and baking soda and add to the batter. Scrape down the sides of the bowl again and mix until the batter is well combined.

Drop cookie dough in one-inch mounds and place them on the baking sheet, about 2 inches apart.

Bake on center rack in oven for 15–17 minutes or until golden brown. Let the cookies cool completely on a wire rack before glazing them.

CHOCOLATE GLAZE

8 ounces semi-sweet chocolate
2 tablespoons sour cream, or more as needed

In a small saucepan over very low heat, melt the chocolate. Combine the melted chocolate and sour cream and mix until smooth. If necessary, add more sour cream to obtain a spreadable consistency. Using a rubber spatula, spread evenly over the top of the cookie or pipe the glaze from a pastry bag for a more interesting look.

Store the cookies in an airtight container.

Yields approximately 2 dozen cookies.

WE MAKE TWO ENTIRELY DIFFERENT GINGER COOKIES. ONE CHEWY (GINGIES), ONE CRUNCHY (DORIS'S), BOTH DELICIOUS. YOU CHOOSE.

DORIS'S GINGER SLICES

DORIS MEDDIN (SHERYL'S MOTHER-IN-LAW) HAS THESE WAITING FOR SHERYL AND STUART EVERY TIME THEY COME FOR A VISIT. THESE COOKIES ARE INCREDIBLY TASTY LITTLE MORSELS. THEY ARE PERFECT WITH A CUP OF COFFEE AND DELICIOUS BROKEN UP OVER VANILLA ICE CREAM.

1/4 pound (1 stick) unsalted butter, room temperature
1/2 cup granulated sugar
1/4 cup dark molasses
1 2/3 cups all-purpose flour
1 tablespoon plus 2 teaspoons ground ginger

1/4 teaspoon ground cloves
1/2 teaspoon ground cinnamon
1/2 teaspoon baking soda
1 1/2 ounces finely chopped crystalized ginger (optional, for real ginger junkies)

Preheat the oven to 350 degrees. Line a baking sheet with parchment paper or grease the sheet well. Set aside.

Using an electric mixer on medium speed, cream butter. Add sugar and mix well. Add molasses and continue mixing until blended. Using a rubber spatula, scrape down the sides of the bowl. In a small bowl, combine flour, ginger, cloves, cinnamon, and baking soda. Add to the mixing bowl and blend well. (If opting for the crystallized ginger, now is the time to stir it in.)

Remove the dough from the mixer and divide it into 4 rolls, each about 1 1/2 inches thick and 10–12 inches long. Roll each log in waxed paper and refrigerate at least one day. (Doris makes these a week in advance!)

When ready to bake, slice each log into 1/8-inch discs and place on baking sheet about 1/2 inch apart.

Bake on center rack in oven for approximately 8 minutes or until dark brown in color. Cool on a wire rack.

Store the cookies in an airtight container.

Yields approximately 150 (itty bitty) cookies.

GINGIES

*T*HESE ARE THE SOFT ONES! CARRIE BAILEY (THE DAUGHTER OF OUR FRIEND CALLIE/CAROLINE) GAVE US THIS RECIPE AND WE CAN'T THANK HER ENOUGH! THEY'RE MORE "GROWN UP" TASTING THAN YOUR TYPICAL COOKIE, SO WE CAN ENJOY THEM AND PROFESS TO BE "ADULTS." BUT KIDS LOVE THEM TOO!

6 ounces (1 1/2 sticks) unsalted butter, room temperature
2 cups granulated sugar
2 large eggs, room temperature
1/2 teaspoon vanilla extract
3/4 cup molasses
2 teaspoons white vinegar
4 cups all-purpose flour
1 1/2 teaspoons baking soda
1 tablespoon plus 1 teaspoon ground ginger
1 teaspoon ground cinnamon
1/2 teaspoon ground cloves

Preheat the oven to 325 degrees. Line a baking sheet with parchment paper or grease the sheet well. Set aside.

Using an electric mixer on medium speed, cream butter. Add sugar and mix well. Add eggs, one at a time, and beat until combined. Using a rubber spatula, scrape down the sides of the bowl. Stir in vanilla extract, molasses, and vinegar. In a small bowl, combine flour, baking soda and spices and stir into the batter, scraping down the sides of the bowl as necessary.

Scoop the cookie dough into 1-inch mounds and place on the baking sheet, approximately 2 inches apart.

Bake on center rack in oven for 10–12 minutes. You'll know they are done when they start to wrinkle on top. Cool on a wire rack.

Store the cookies in an airtight container.

Yields approximately 3 dozen cookies.

Scrape the sides and bottom of the mixing bowl several times while making a batter. It helps to thoroughly combine all of the ingredients.

LOVELY LOIS'S LUSCIOUS LEMON LEGACIES

◇

OVELY LOIS (BENNETT'S GODMOTHER) HAS ALWAYS BAKED THESE COOKIES TO SATISFY HER OWN LUST FOR LEMONS. LOIS LOVES LEMONS. WE LOVE LOIS'S LEMON COOKIES.

6 ounces (1 1/2 sticks) unsalted butter, room temperature
1 cup granulated sugar
1 large egg, room temperature
1 1/2 teaspoons vanilla extract
Rinds of 2 large lemons, grated
1/4 cup fresh lemon juice
2 1/2 cups all-purpose flour
1 1/2 teaspoons baking powder
1/2 teaspoon baking soda
1/2 teaspoon salt

Preheat the oven to 350 degrees. Line a baking sheet with parchment paper or grease the sheet well. Set aside.

Using an electric mixer on medium speed, cream butter. Add sugar and continue beating on medium speed until blended. Add egg, vanilla extract, lemon rind, and lemon juice. Mix well, using a rubber spatula to scrape down the sides of the bowl. In a small bowl combine flour, baking powder, baking soda, and salt and add to the batter. Mix on low speed until well blended, scraping down the sides of the bowl as necessary.

Using a teaspoon, scoop the dough onto the baking sheet, about 2 inches apart.

Bake on center rack in oven for 15 minutes or until edges turn golden. Cool on a wire rack.

Store the cookies in an airtight container.

Yields approximately 55 large or 80 small cookies.

Note: These cookies are really adorable when you scoop them with a half-teaspoon measure. Watch the baking time, though. They will not take nearly as long!

AUNT DOTTIE'S MERINGUE COOKIES

*T*HESE COOKIES WERE EVERYWHERE WHILE BENNETT WAS GROWING UP IN CHARLESTON, SOUTH CAROLINA. BUT SHE SWEARS HER AUNT DOTTIE'S WERE THE BEST.

3 large egg whites, room temperature
1/2 teaspoon salt
1 cup granulated sugar
1 cup sweetened coconut
1 1/2 cups pecan pieces
1/2 cup golden raisins
1 teaspoon vanilla extract
1/2 teaspoon almond extract

Preheat the oven to 325 degrees. Line a baking sheet with parchment paper or grease the sheet well. Set aside.

Using an electric mixer on high speed, beat egg whites with salt until almost stiff. Continue beating egg whites, gradually adding sugar. In a small bowl, combine coconut, pecans, and raisins and fold them into the egg whites, mixing as little as possible. Stir in vanilla and almond extracts.

Drop heaping teaspoons of the dough onto the baking sheet, approximately 2 inches apart.

Bake on center rack in oven for about 20 minutes or until the cookies are golden brown. Cool on a wire rack.

Store the cookies in an airtight container.

Yields approximately 4 dozen cookies.

THUMBPRINT COOKIES

WE BOTH LOVED MAKING THESE COOKIES AS KIDS. REMEMBER HOW YOU USED YOUR THUMB TO MAKE THE PRINT TO FILL WITH JAM? KIDS STILL LOVE MAKING THESE!

1/4 pound (1 stick) unsalted butter, room temperature
1/2 cup granulated sugar
1/2 teaspoon vanilla extract
1 large egg, separated and room temperature
1 cup all-purpose flour
1/4 teaspoon salt
1 1/2 cups finely chopped pecan pieces
Approximately 1 cup raspberry preserves

Preheat the oven to 350 degrees. Line a baking sheet with parchment paper or grease the sheet well. Set aside.

Using an electric mixer on medium speed, cream butter. Add sugar and vanilla extract and continue beating until the batter is light and fluffy, about 5 minutes. Add egg yolk and blend well. In a small bowl, combine flour and salt and add to the batter. Scrape down the sides of the bowl with a rubber spatula and mix well.

Roll the dough into walnut-size balls. Dip each ball into the egg white and then roll it in the pecan pieces. Place each ball on the cookie sheet and make a "thumbprint" indentation in each cookie. Fill each "print" with approximately 1 teaspoon of raspberry jam.

Bake on center rack in oven for 20–25 minutes or until the cookies are golden brown. Cool on a wire rack.

Store the cookies in an airtight container.

Yields approximately 20 cookies.

FRUITCAKE COOKIES

OK. YOU HATE FRUITCAKE, TOO. BUT WE SWEAR, JUST TRY THESE. WE WERE JUST AS SKEPTICAL WHEN ELLEN FRISCH (BENNETT'S SISTER-IN-LAW) INSISTED WE GIVE THEM A GO. YOU'RE GOING TO LOVE THEM. THEY'RE A SOPHISTICATED TOUCH TO YOUR HOLIDAY COOKIE PLATTER.

2 1/2 cups all-purpose flour
1/4 teaspoon cream of tartar
1/2 teaspoon salt
1/2 pound (2 sticks) unsalted butter, room temperature
1 cup confectioners' sugar
1 large egg, room temperature
1 teaspoon vanilla extract
1 cup red candied cherries, coarsely chopped
1 cup green candied cherries, coarsely chopped
1 2/3 cups pecan pieces

Preheat the oven to 375 degrees. Line a baking sheet with parchment paper or grease the sheet well. Set aside.

In a bowl, combine flour, cream of tartar, and salt and set aside. Using an electric mixer on medium speed, cream butter and add sugar, beating until well mixed. Add egg and vanilla extract and beat until light and fluffy, about 5 minutes. On low speed, gradually add the dry ingredients, scraping down the sides of the bowl with a rubber spatula and beating only until mixed. Using a wooden spoon (or your hands), mix in the fruit and pecan pieces.

Form the dough into 4 logs, each approximately 1 inch thick and 10 inches long. Wrap the dough in waxed paper and refrigerate at least 8 hours.

Slice the dough into 1/4-inch-thick rounds and place on the baking sheet, about 1 inch apart.

Bake on center rack in oven for 13–15 minutes or until the edges and bottoms of the cookies are golden brown. The cookies should not brown on the top. Cool on a wire rack.

Store the cookies in an airtight container.

Yields 6–7 dozen cookies.

THOSE COOKIES

WE PONDERED FOR HOURS OVER WHAT TO CALL "THOSE" COOKIES WITH THE WHITE CHOCOLATE AND MACADAMIA NUTS . . . .

5 ounces (1 1/4 sticks) unsalted butter, room temperature
1/2 cup granulated sugar
1/3 cup light brown sugar, packed
2 large eggs, room temperature
1 teaspoon vanilla extract
2 cups all-purpose flour
1 teaspoon baking soda
3/4 teaspoon salt
8 ounces white chocolate, broken into small pieces
2/3 cup chopped macadamia nuts (about 3 ounces)

Preheat the oven to 350 degrees. Line a baking sheet with parchment paper or grease the sheet well. Set aside.

Using an electric mixer on medium speed, cream butter. Add sugars and beat until well blended. Add eggs, one at a time, scraping down the sides of the bowl with a rubber spatula and continue mixing until the batter is light and fluffy, about 5 minutes. Add vanilla extract. In a small bowl, combine flour, baking soda, and salt and gradually add to the batter. Stir in white chocolate and macadamia nuts.

Scoop tablespoon-size mounds onto the baking sheet, approximately 2 inches apart.

Bake on center rack in oven for 15 minutes or until the cookies are golden brown. Let cool on a wire rack.

Store the cookies in an airtight container.

Yields approximately 3 dozen cookies.

Welcome
to the
neighborhood

RECIPES

Callie's/Caroline's "Provisional" Brownies

~⌒~

EVERYONE ELSE CALLS HER CALLIE, BUT WE CALL HER CAROLINE. REGARDLESS OF WHAT YOU CALL HER, CAROLINE WHITE IS A TRULY OUTRAGEOUS COOK, AND HER FUDGY BROWNIES PROVE IT.

4 ounces unsweetened chocolate
1/4 pound (1 stick) unsalted butter
3 large eggs, room temperature
2 teaspoons vanilla extract
2 cups granulated sugar
1/2 teaspoon salt
1 cup all-purpose flour
1 cup chopped walnuts

Preheat the oven to 350 degrees. Prepare a 9 x 13 x 2-inch pan by greasing it, lining it with parchment paper, and greasing the paper. Then flour the pan, tapping out excess flour. Set aside.

In a small saucepan over very low heat, melt chocolate and butter together and let cool. Using an electric mixer on high speed, combine eggs, vanilla extract, sugar, and salt, and mix for 8–10 minutes. Batter will be lemon yellow in color. On low speed, add chocolate/butter mixture. Stir in the flour, scraping down the sides of the bowl with a rubber spatula. Stir in walnut pieces.

Pour the batter into the pan and bake on center rack in oven for 40 minutes or until just firm in the center. Let the brownies cool completely on a wire rack before cutting.

Store the brownies at room temperature.

Yields approximately 24 brownies.

BETTY'S BROWNIES

WHEN ALICE LEVKOFF, OF CHARLESTON, SOUTH CAROLINA, SERVED HER FRIEND BETTY'S BROWNIES AT HER DAUGHTER'S ENGAGEMENT PARTY, THEY DISAPPEARED BEFORE SHERYL EVEN HAD A CHANCE TO TASTE THEM. ALICE WAS KIND ENOUGH TO MAKE THEM AGAIN FOR SHERYL LATER IN THE WEEK. IT'S NO WONDER THESE FUDGY BROWNIES WERE DEVOURED SO QUICKLY.

- 4 ounces unsweetened chocolate
- 6 ounces (1 1/2 sticks) unsalted butter
- 4 large eggs, room temperature
- 2 cups granulated sugar
- 1 teaspoon vanilla extract
- 1/2 teaspoon salt
- 1 cup all-purpose flour
- 1 cup pecan pieces

Preheat the oven to 325 degrees. Grease a 9 x 13 x 2-inch pan. Set aside.

In a small saucepan over very low heat, melt chocolate and butter together and set aside. Using an electric mixer on medium speed, beat eggs and add sugar, mixing well. Add vanilla extract and salt, scraping down the sides of the bowl with a rubber spatula. Add flour and mix until combined. Add chocolate and butter mixture, scraping down the sides of the bowl again, and mix on low speed until blended. Stir in the pecan pieces.

Pour the batter into the pan and bake on center rack in oven for 20–25 minutes or until the batter is set. Do not overbake. Let the brownies cool completely on a wire rack before cutting.

Store the brownies at room temperature.

Yields approximately 2 dozen brownies.

BLONDE BROWNIES

WE DEVELOPED THIS RECIPE AROUND THE TIME IT WAS ANNOUNCED THAT THE 1996 OLYMPICS WOULD BE HELD IN ATLANTA. TO RECOGNIZE THIS HONOR, WE NAMED THESE "OLYMPIC BLONDE BROWNIES." UNFORTUNATELY, A SHORT WHILE LATER, ACOG (ATLANTA COMMITTEE FOR THE OLYMPIC GAMES) NOTIFIED US THAT WE WERE NOT PERMITTED TO USE THE WORD "OLYMPIC" IN THIS MANNER. RATHER THAN HIRE A LAWYER, WE CHANGED THE NAME. BUT THESE BROWNIES ARE STILL WORTHY OF A GOLD MEDAL.

1/4 pound (1 stick) unsalted butter, room temperature
1 1/4 cups light brown sugar, packed
2 large eggs, room temperature
1 1/4 cups all-purpose flour
3/4 teaspoon salt
3/4 teaspoon vanilla extract
1 cup pecan pieces
8 ounces white chocolate, broken into small pieces

Preheat the oven to 350 degrees. Grease a 9 x 13 x 2-inch pan. Set aside.

Using an electric mixer, cream butter. Add brown sugar and beat until fluffy. Add eggs, one at a time, and continue beating on medium speed until well mixed, about 5 minutes. Using a rubber spatula, scrape down the sides of the bowl and add the flour, salt, and vanilla extract. Mix well. Add pecan pieces and white chocolate and mix until blended.

Pour the batter into the greased pan and bake on center rack in oven for approximately 30 minutes or until golden brown and just firm in the middle. Do not overbake. If you can stand the wait, let the brownies cool completely on a wire rack before slicing. They'll be much neater!

Store the brownies at room temperature.

Yields approximately 2 dozen brownies.

WHITAKERS

SOME PEOPLE CALL THESE A "SEVEN LAYER" COOKIE. SOME PEOPLE CALL THEM "HELLO DOLLIES." WE NAMED THEM AFTER OUR DUMPSTER COMPANY, WHITAKER AND SONS, BECAUSE, IN ESSENCE, ALL YOU DO IS DUMP THESE INGREDIENTS INTO A PAN. EASY AND GOOD!

1/4 pound (1 stick) unsalted butter, melted and cooled
1 1/2 cups graham cracker crumbs
2 1/4 cups pecan pieces
1 1/2 cups semi-sweet chocolate chips
1 1/2 cups butterscotch chips
1 1/2 cups sweetened coconut
1 1/2 cans (21 ounces) sweetened condensed milk

Preheat the oven to 350 degrees. Grease a 9 x 13 x 2-inch pan. Set aside.

Melt the butter and pour it evenly into the pan.
Sprinkle the graham cracker crumbs evenly over the melted butter.
Sprinkle the pecans evenly over the graham cracker crumbs.
Sprinkle the chocolate chips evenly over the pecans.
Sprinkle the butterscotch chips evenly over the chocolate chips.
Sprinkle the coconut evenly over the butterscotch chips.
Pour the condensed milk evenly over the top.

Bake on center rack in oven for 30–35 minutes or until the top is set and nicely browned. Let the Whitakers cool completely on a wire rack before slicing.

Store the Whitakers at room temperature.

Yields approximately 2 dozen Whitakers.

LEMON SQUARES

OUR FRIEND, JOHN GRAHAM, WON'T EAT ANYTHING ORANGE (CARROTS, YAMS, CANTALOUPES). BUT HE OBVIOUSLY DOESN'T HAVE THE SAME AVERSION TO YELLOW, BECAUSE HE LOVES THESE LEMON SQUARES.

CRUST
1/2 pound (2 sticks) unsalted butter, room temperature
2 1/4 cups all-purpose flour
1/2 cup confectioners' sugar
Rind of 1 large lemon, grated

Preheat the oven to 325 degrees. Grease a 9 x 13 x 2-inch baking pan. Set aside.

Using an electric mixer on medium speed, cream butter. On low speed, add the flour, sugar, and lemon rind. Mix until well blended. Do not whip!

Pour the crust into the prepared pan and distribute evenly. Bake on center rack in oven for 25 minutes or until golden brown. Set aside.

FILLING
4 large eggs, room temperature　　*6 tablespoons lemon juice*
2 cups granulated sugar　　*1/2 teaspoon vanilla extract*
Grated rind of 1 large lemon　　*1/2 teaspoon baking powder*

Using an electric mixer on high speed, beat eggs and sugar together until thickened, about 5 minutes. Add lemon rind, lemon juice, vanilla extract, and baking powder. Scrape down the sides of the bowl with a rubber spatula and mix well.

Pour the lemon mixture over the baked crust and bake on center rack in oven for 40 minutes, or until the filling is set. These lemon squares need to cool completely on a wire rack before serving or they don't cut "gracefully."

Store the lemon squares in the refrigerator, but bring them to room temperature before serving. Dust with confectioners' sugar for a more finished look.

Yields approximately 2 dozen squares.

CHRIS'S FABULOUS FUDGE

WHEN CHRIS KESTLE-KAUFMAN GAVE US THIS FUDGE FOR CHRISTMAS ONE YEAR, WE HOARDED IT TO AVOID HAVING TO SHARE ANY. WE THEN HAD THE NERVE TO CALL AND BEG THE RECIPE FROM HER. THANKS FOR SHARING, CHRIS! THAT'S WHAT FRIENDS ARE FOR.

2 cups granulated sugar
2/3 cup evaporated milk
12 large marshmallows
1/4 pound (1 stick) unsalted butter
1/2 teaspoon salt
1 cup semi-sweet chocolate chips
1 teaspoon vanilla extract
1 cup chopped walnuts or pecans (optional)

Using butter, grease an 8-inch square pan. Set aside.

In a heavy 2-quart saucepan, combine sugar, evaporated milk, marshmallows, butter, and salt. Cook, stirring constantly, over medium heat until the mixture comes to a boil. The mixture MUST bubble all over the top. At this point, boil and stir for 5 minutes more. (This is a *critical* step. Do not skimp on the time!) Remove from heat. Stir in the chocolate chips and vanilla extract. Continue stirring until the chips are melted. Stir in the chopped nuts, if desired.

Spread the fudge into the prepared pan. Cool completely on a wire rack before serving.

Store the fudge at room temperature.

Yields approximately 4 dozen pieces.

INDEX

Index

BROWNIES AND BARS

IT'S A FUNNY THING ABOUT BROWNIES AND BARS. IF YOU LEAVE A FULL PAN OUT ON THE COUNTER, SOMEONE IS GOING TO CUT INTO IT. (AND THEN SOMEONE ELSE, AND THEN SOMEONE ELSE AND SOMEONE ELSE.) BECAUSE OF THEIR FORMAT, THEY ARE EITHER THE DIETER'S DELIGHT OR DOWNFALL. (AFTER ALL, ONE LITTLE SLIVER OF FUDGE CERTAINLY CAN'T HURT.) WILLPOWER ASIDE, BROWNIES AND BARS OFFER THE OPTION OF CUSTOM-SIZED PORTIONS.

BROWNIES AND BARS ALSO OFFER THE ADVANTAGE OF PORTABILITY. THIS MIGHT BE ONE OF THE REASONS THAT THEY SHOW UP AT SO MANY PICNICS. NOT ONLY DO PEOPLE LOVE THEM, BUT IT'S ALSO EASY TO GET THEM THERE.

SINCE BROWNIES AND BARS ARE SO "PACKABLE," THEY MAKE GREAT ADDITIONS TO YOUR CUSTOM BASKETS AND DECORATIVE TINS. WHAT TEACHER OR NEIGHBOR WOULDN'T BE DELIGHTED WITH THIS GIFT?

IT'S HARD TO IMAGINE A MORE VERSATILE DESSERT, BAR NONE!